Dock Brown

Outlaw of Grayson County Kentucky

William R. Haynes

Dock Brown
*Outlaw of Grayson County
Kentucky*

William R. Haynes

COMMONWEALTH BOOK COMPANY
St. Martin, Ohio
2017

© 2017 by Commonwealth Book Company.
All rights reserved.

CHAPTER I (Introductory)

On the twenty-second day of January, in the year of our Lord, eighteen hundred and seventy-five, the spot known to the neighborhood as "The Brown Graves" was visited by one to whom it has long been familiar. There are only two sunken mounds upon the high, rocky hill which overlooks the beautiful valley, sentineled by the picturesque Pine Knob, in the western part of Grayson County, Kentucky, three miles north of the thriving village of Caneyville. Leaning over the sunken graves are two rude monuments bearing these inscriptions:

JOHN * BROWN
Was born October 17, 1776,
and departed this life
May 27, 1848

P. H. BROWN
Born November 18th, 1816
Departed this life
February 1, 1848

There is a smooth, round niche between the Christian and surname on the first stone, as indicated by the asterisk as a substitute for an initial letter—which seems to have been "picked in" after the lettering had been completed. What that missing letter was will appear in the course of this narrative. A quarter of an acre of ground was cleared off for this rural cemetery about twenty-five years ago, but the picket fence that originally enclosed it had rotted down, and nothing remains of it but a few worm-eaten and weather bleached pickets and the ends of two logs to which they are nailed, resting upon two large sandstones. The place is again forest-grown, and presents a picture of perfect abandonment. The hill crowned by the neglected and abandonend graveyard rises to the height of three hundred feet above the old log cabin and church and broomsedge field in the valley at its foot.

Standing upon this elevation, among the scrubby saplings of oak, sassafras and sour-wood, one forgets his relation to the busy world as he is overwhelmed with the blended beauty, sublimity and grandeur of the scenery. A few feet fronting westward are two or three large rocks covered with a heavy carpet of green and yellow moss, so soft and clean and inviting that one cannot resist the impulse to stoop and caress it with the palm of his hand. These rocks are the apex of the hill, and jut over a steep declivity, which,

with irregular step-stones, terminates many hundred feet below in a deep and rugged gorge. But far above the tops of the tall timber below, the eye is carried to the blue, rolling hills miles beyond, which seem to climb heavenward in majestic rivalry to secure the parting rays of the descending sun. To the left are the tall, gray cliffs or rugged old Pine Knob—solid walls of granite full one hundred and fifty feet from base to brink—crowned with the eternal verdure of the evergreens and the majesty of noble forest kings, whose leaves rustle to the kiss of every breeze, and among the greenery song birds hold constant concert, while the clear waves of the winding, babbling streamlet at its base
"Dance to the music of their melodies
And sparkle in their brightness."
The cliff-sides are full of caverns, from stock-shelter below to eagles' eyries and ravens' nests above. In the floors of the cave are Indian mortars in which the aborigines pounded their maize. There are also horse, mule, sheep, deer and turkey tracks in the solid rock as plainly visible as though newly made in the plastic clay. The largest of these excavations is locally known as "Dick's Tobacco Barn," from the fact that Dick Galloway once housed his crop of tobacco therein. Far up on the shelves of this cave and of its companion, Big Mouth, vultures build their nests and hatch their young undisturbed. Indeed, Pine Knob has been a home and shelter for nearly every species of animated creation, from the genus Homo to the genus Falco. And, if you, dear reader, have any admiration for these things which are inspiringly beautiful in nature to behold and enrapturing to hear, go to Pine Knob in the early springtime, when the wild buds are bursting, and every woodland songster has tuned his blithest notes in harmony with the entrancing scenes as well as with the bell-like music of the silvery jet-d'eau which shimmeringly leaps from an everlasting spring upon the south side, as pure and pellucid as the tears of Pieria which formed the Parnassian spring, the glory of the gods and the primal fountain of poesy among men! Go and drink in with your eyes all the beauty, and glory, and grandeur, and sublimity unborn of the indescribable panorama of mountain, hill, forest, vale, river, cliff, cavern, and dark, deep gorge! Go there and drink into your soul the awe-born thought that "This is not earth—this is not the work of man—surely God has been here!" But, if you have no ear for music, no eye for the beautiful; if you have never felt an indescribable yet pleasant thrill on the flesh as the inner man expanded at the thought of things sublime, go not thou there!

Outlaw of Grayson County

To finish the picture of this famous locality it is necessary to state that the broken stone walls of the dairy, near the spring, are there as they were eighteen years ago; and the old log meeting-house erected by the neighbors and candidates in eighteen hundred and thirty-seven, is also standing. Charles Stuteville, a Regular Baptist minister from Nolin, in the eastern part of the county, was the first preacher who took charge of the congregation there. He preached once a month to large audiences, notwithstanding the country was sparsely settled. The worshippers came from ten to twelve miles around, men and women of piety, sobriety and religious zeal; not with broadcloth coats, cassimer pants, high silk hats, morocco boots, but flax or jean pants, home-spun hats, and shoes in winter, and in summer the latter were generally nature-spun. The women had not the silks, delains and status of these days, but were content with calico and linsey for Sunday, in winter, and checked cotton for summer every-day wear. Their shoes were also made at home but were too fine and dear for summer, except on church Sundays, and then they were carried in the hand until in sight of the meeting-house. Many of the best young women would walk two or three miles to their regular church-meeting, rather than burden the tired horses that pulled the plow during the week.

This church was the place of meeting and worship for the people on Short Creek and Caney, which includes an area of about twenty-five miles square. All within this boundary were truly neighbors and knew nothing and practiced nothing in their dealings but plain, unassuming honesty. The distress or suffering of one was felt to some extent by all. They had plenty to eat, drink and wear. Those blessed with health were happy. If a discordant note was struck in one locality, it reverberated with effect through the whole. Strangers were lodged and fed for thanks. Any innovation on this was a gross violation of conventional usage, and a disgrace to the party thus offending.

This was society proper, but there were bad men and, possibly, bad women in that community as in all others. But these, for their debauchery and neglect of person, are generally a surplusage upon the outskirts of unsocial obscurity, and unworthy of mention in the above connection.

Such is Pine Knob. Such was the state of society there until the desecration of its hallowed precincts in the year eighteen hundred and forty-one in the manner to be detailed in the following:

CHAPTER II. The Murder in the Woods

About the close of the year eighteen hundred and twenty-five, a man named Gulliam Hopper, living in the County of Warren, State of Tennessee, located a piece of land adjoining his home tract, upon which latter he had been living a number of years. Te and his family had come originally from one of the Gulf states. Of their antecedents their most intimate acquaintances knew nothing; yet they were received with welcome and regarded as good neighbors. Hopper was a man of industrious habits, miserly economy, rash and inflexible temper. And these qualities were greatly strengthened and permanently developed by a sensitiveness arising from the knowledge of his neglected children. His language was bad, his speech was short. When he gave offense, he felt the lashings of conscience, and often made atonement for the injury by some unexpected, extraordinary kindness. Such disposition is nearly always the companion of excitable temperaments. The so-called even, quiet temper is less repentant, and seldom forgiving. Which is the better? Readers, decide. The former, in a moment, may destroy life; the latter, happiness. Hopper was, however, a strange and singular mixture of disposition. Whilst he was quiet in the endeavor to right his own wrongs—in this particular he was forgiving—he would never mantle the wrongs of others. His wife, whose name was Nancy, was of a class of women one seldom meets. She had a soul full of filial love and domestic care. As her being was merged into that of her husband, she became the principal factor of his better nature, uncomplainingly serving at the altar of self-sacrifice, demonstrating no sorrow of her own further than sympathetic words in her administrations to those of whose entity she was a part. Aside from her devotion to family interests, her serenity of temperament and frequent and unostentatious charity won for her the confidence and esteem of her whole circle of acquaintances; all of whom as an acknowledgement of her many admirable graces, addressed her as "Aunt Nancy." Her education was limited but she could read. This, however, was a recreation in which she seldom engaged further than a few chapters in the family Bible. A member of the church, she seldom attended divine worship, owing to the burden of household duties, made heavy by a numerous family of children, consisting of seven boys and two girls. Those who were large enough were required by their father to work upon the farm during the crop season, which was about nine months of the year, and to attend school (when there was one) the remaining three months.

Outlaw of Grayson County

As some of these children will play prominent parts in this story, it is but proper to designate them by name in order of their ages, beginning with the eldest. They were Moses, Annie, Samuel, James, William M., Pinkney, Absalom, Gulliam and Polly. Such a force on a southern farm of size and fertility could but rapidly bring prosperity in the accumulation of wealth.

Hopper soon began to realize his importance in the community as a citizen and taxpayer; but, like most men of his temperament who first begin, at the age of forty, to realize their ability to be useful in their neighborhood, he became snappish and proscriptive. He desired that people should yield to his opinion on all questions pertaining to the subject of livestock and lands. Having enjoyed possession of the land he had warranted for four years, he began to speak of it as his own, and cut timber and clear.

Early in the spring of eighteen hundred and twenty-nine, he and two of the boys had gone to the woods to rive boards. He took his gun along, and finding a suitable tree, he put the boys to chopping, and went to his dog that had treed a squirrel but a short distance over the hill. Twenty minutes after, the gun fired. The boys paused a few seconds then worked on. Had they waited a few moments longer they might have seen a young man of their acquaintance, affrighted and white-faced, beating a rapid retreat from the direction in which they heard the report of their father's gun. Hopper soon came hurrying to them, pale and trembling.

"O, God! my dear boys," he exclaimed, "I've killed old Stockstill! God have mercy! Run home quick and tell Nancy to fetch Kit to the big root-wad in the holler! Goodbye! I won't see you no more! Tell her to come tonight at nine o'clock!"

The man then disappeared in the forest.

The boys stood by the tree, open-mouthed and wondering. Their eyes met. Up to this time they had not fully realized the awful meaning of their father's words. The shirt-sleeves of the younger were soon wet with tears. They were suddenly aroused from their apathy of terror by a solemn wail from the dying man. Running home without pause, their sad story was soon told.

Henry Skelton was the young man who retreated when the gun fired. He ran directly to the village, not over a mile distant, and imparted the following history of the deed of blood to the local magistrate:

"Mr. Stockstill and myself went over to survey a piece of woodland which I had proposed to purchase. It was near Hopper's place. We set the compass upon the bearing indicated and run the line, and as we were locating the corner, Mr. Hopper approached us with a rifle-gun on his shoulder. We spoke to him, but making no reply, he asked:

" 'What in the hell are you doing on my land?'

" 'We are not on your land, sir. This is my land, if you please.'

" 'You are a damned liar!' was the reply. Stockstill seemed to grow very angry, but I told him to say nothing more; not to have difficulty and to come away.

" 'No,' said he 'this is my soil. I am on it and will not be driven away. I am not afraid of his gun.'

"Hopper, stepping back a few feet, drew his gun to his shoulder, saying, 'Damn you, I'll show you,' or something of that kind. What Mr. Stockstill then said I do not recollect. I cried to Hopper not to shoot, that we would leave. He fired. Mr. Stockstill fell. Hopper advanced toward me, and I left."

Upon this information a warrant of arrest was issued, and a party started in pursuit of the murderer.

The coroner with his jury, the bereaved family of Stockstill, Skelton, and a few others, came that night to the spot where the dead man lay. The cold light of a half-moon was broken and obscured by trees and undergrowth, whose dark shadows fell upon the stark and lifeless form. A light-wood torch cast a brilliant blaze, disclosing the position of the dead man lying prone in a pool of gore, by his side his broken compass. Examination of the body revealed a large bullet hole through the chest, the undeniable cause of death. The statement of Skelton, in substance the same as that made to the magistrate, was repeated to the jury, who rendered this:

VERDICT

We, of the jury, find that the deceased, David Stockstill, came to his death from a shotgun wound at the hands of Gulliam Hopper, on the twentieth day of April, eighteen hundred and twenty-nine.

J. Frost, Foreman.

David Stockstill was an influential and highly respected citizen. His remains were neatly coffined and interred in the nearby graveyard.

CHAPTER III. Flight of the Murderer

Imagination can well picture the painful effect produced upon the household by the broken and tearful utterances of the two boys as they entered the yard-gate. The poor brush of words upon such a picture can make but feeble strokes to call sympathy to the shrine of misery.

Ten hours at length wore away; but their plowshare of sorrowful moments traced furrows of gloom in one life never to be effaced. Hours are weeks, and minutes days to blighted happiness and agonizing suspense. "Time is a measured portion of duration," it is said. But by what is it measured—the heavenly bodies—a clock—a watch? These do for uniformity and computation, but they are not the true measure. The true measure is the cup of life placed in the hand of each one at his birth and filled at his death. Some fill early, some late. When all shall have been filled, then time will be no more!

Long ere night the money-drawer was opened, and four hundred dollars in silver and gold placed in a small bag. Kit, the favorite riding horse that had been grazing upon the young pasture, was hitched in the strip of woods near the stable. Moses, who had been married two years, was living to himself upon the home farm. He had been informed of the tragic occurrence, and with his wife and little boy had come to his mother. His advice was for all to remain at the house except mother and Polly, the babe. This course was agreed upon, and the mother and child were in the act of starting when a rap was heard at the front door. All were silent within. Another knock, and Moses asked:

"Who is that?"

"Some friends from town. We will do you no harm," was the response.

Moses opened the door. The sheriff and his posse entered the house. The former asked for Hopper.

"He is not here," said Moses.

Mrs. Hopper trembling, told them that Mr. Hopper had gone away that morning and had not yet returned. Gulliam said, "Ma, I told you that Pa had——." The mother shook her head and the boy lapsed into silence.

The house and premises were searched, and the men left. The horses had been left some distance from the house in charge of one of the men. They reached them, and after a brief and whispered consultation, concluded to guard the premises during the remainder of the night. They mounted and each took his station about fifty yards from the house. They were discovered by Moses who had anticipated this design.

How the money and horses were to be conveyed to Hopper was a perplexing question.

Mrs. Hopper, with a milk pail in her hand and the money in her bosom, accompanied by one of the boys, started to the stable. The guard intercepted her but seeing the pail and hearing her statement that she had not milked the cows, permitted her to pass. A few steps and she was at the stable, beyond the calf lot and by the side of the patient horse. A quarter of a mile brought them to the root-wad, the place of meeting—and parting. The croaking frogs in the calamus swamp nearby hushed at their approach. All was still as the grave. Hopper was close at hand, but as it was cloudy and dark, he could not recognize their forms and remained in concealment until he heard his wife's voice breathing his name. He then emerged from the thicket, and they met.

She told him of the guard at the house, her plan to escape, and of a speedy return, in order to avoid arousing suspicion. Filling his pockets with dried beef and biscuit from the piggin, for the thoughtful creature had calculated all his needs, she gave him the money. He started to count it but was stopped by the sudden thought of pursuers.

"Nancy, I'm in an awful fix. I've got to go off and leave everything on earth that I love. If we ever see each other any more, I hope I'll be a better man, and that we have forgot what I have done, and how sorry I am now. My boy, be good and try to forget what your daddy has done."

The man and horse disappeared over the hill, and the sound of the swiftly receding hoofs died away in the distance ere the mother and son broke the silence of their desertion and loneliness and started home. They reached the house without discovery, and all was well.

At one o'clock that night, or rather the next morning, the stable guard was awakened by his companions, and all of them departed for their several homes after the sheriff had appointed a time and place for their reassembling.

A few weeks after the events just described, a reward of five hundred dollars was offered by the Governor of Tennessee for the apprehension and conviction of Gulliam Hopper, the alleged murderer of David Stockstill.

In those days mails were conveyed from one end of the country to the other on horseback, and news items of the most interesting and vital character were considered early in the interior when two weeks old. Now they are quite stale when two days old. Then a murder sent a shock through an entire state. Now it is unnoticed beyond the county in which it is committed, and forgotten in a week. The outrage then upon justice and human sympathies, the broad gash in the quiet of society, called for, and generally obtained, united and ready action upon the part of the people in the vindication of the law, which was at least equal to the work of today, with all our boasted facilities of railroad, photography, telegraph and newspapers.

Aside from the inducements presented by the offer of reward, the personal interests of every good citizen of Warren County prompted a most vigilant and ready action toward the arrest. The relatives of Stockstill spared neither time nor money in their efforts to pursue and capture Hopper. Night after night his premises were surrounded by bodies of armed men. Often was the rumor afloat that he had been thereabouts. Months, however, passed away, and nothing reliable had been heard of him. Excitement subsided, and the people resumed their usual vocations with apparent apathy respecting the murder.

CHAPTER IV. At the Salt-Works—Further Flight

Shortly after the separation from his wife and son as detailed in the preceding chapter, Hopper rapidly retreated along a stock path which, with many windings, terminated miles away in the heart of the lowlands of a dark and wilderness region. After a few hours of rapid riding he paused, dismounted, and seated himself upon a log to rest and mature his future plans.

The purse of money was heavy and sorely weighted the side upon which he had been carrying it. He separated it into several lots, and deposited one in each of the pockets of his coat and pants. Then he partook of the lunch provided by his thoughtful wife, and feeling refreshed, mounted his horse and again pushed on. The echo of his horse's hoofs penetrated the lairs of wolves and panthers which responded with answering howls and screams. But he felt no fear, knowing that his trusty rifle would afford him ample protection against wild beasts. And all through the night, in the midst of the almost trackless forest, the fugitive rode, neither halting nor drawing rein, alone with his thoughts—and, mayhap, haunted by the shape of the man he had slain in the woods.

It was nearing daybreak when, as he approached the great thoroughfare and highway which led from McMinnville to Loy's Cross Roads, he discovered a rail fence which inclosed a cultivated field. It was the first settlement he had seen since his departure, although fully forty miles from home, and the sight filled his soul with terror. What if intelligence of his crime had preceded him, and he should be recognized? Why fear, had he not his rifle to defend himself from arrest? Still as a statue he sat for a moment as these thoughts ran through his mind. It seemed that the very rails were silent, and that every knot held an eye that glared recognition. Even the cool morning breeze appeared to be whispering his secret to the leaves. Suddenly the loud, shrill crowing of a cock in the adjacent barnyard aroused him to action. Looking about him, he saw in the fast brightening dawn a farm house. He said to himself: "Why these fears? Have I turned coward at this time of life? I am a stranger to this place. My horse is tired and hungry. I'll go to the house. My name is Smith."

He turned into the highway, reached the mouth of the lane leading to the dwelling, and rode up to the yard-gate. A dim and flickering light from a greasy lamp in the window indicated that the family were already up. His halloo was answered by a large dog which rushed madly out of the gate. A voice from the door caused the animal to skulk back to his kennel.

"Who lives here, ma'am?" he asked.

"John Hatfield, sir," replied the woman.

"Is he at home, ma'am?" again he queried.

"No, sir," was the response. "He went over to see about Uncle David's being killed. You've heard about that, haven't you?"

"Uncle David who, ma'am?"

"Why, Uncle David Stockstill. What on earth are you a-thinking about? Don't you know Uncle David?"

"Y-e-s—or no, ma'am, I don't know him. I am a stranger in these parts and have been lost."

"What is your name?"

"My name is Smith, ma'am."

"Well, upon my word! Won't you light?"

"No, ma'am, I believe not. Good morning, ma'am."

The horse was reined about, the man continued his journey for parts unknown.

Nothing worthy of note occurred until he reached Sparta, a small village on the Clinch River, and twenty-two miles distant from Hatfield's. He sold his gun and fixtures to the landlord and departed

Outlaw of Grayson County

unsuspected. After a week's travel he reached the Salt Lick, on the Virginia line.

This was a spot to which more people resorted than any other in southwestern Virginia. In fact, it supplied nearly every family with salt in what is known as West Virginia and southern Old Virginia. Many, too, repaired thither from eastern and southern Kentucky and east Tennessee with sacks and wagons for the indispensable mineral.

Hopper, alias Smith, now became John Hooper. Under this name he got employment as a hand at the salt-works. Being stout, ready, and industrious, his wages were increased at the end of the first week, and he soon became a valuable hand in management as well as physical labor.

Months elapsed. He had made no change in, or addition to, his clothing. The money he had brought from home he buried in the woods. No draft was made upon it for even the necessities of life. His wages were barely sufficient for these. His general deportment drew the eyes of suspicion upon him. Sometimes he would absent himself to unknown parts, and upon his return give unsatisfactory explanations of his whereabouts and business. And then he always wore his hat while at work, and pulled down so as to conceal as much of his face as possible. He never had anything to say to traders and visitors. But his position was one of importance, and his employers were charitable enough to construe his actions as eccentricities. He remained for ten months, receiving his wages at the end of each week. In all this time no letters came to him. One day while at work a man approached him and said:

"Well, sir, it seems to me that I have seen you before."

"I reckon not," was Hopper's reply, as he turned away.

The man's name was Dorsey, and he was the landlord of the inn at Sparta where Hooper had stopped nearly a year before when flying from the scene of his crime. Whether the recognition was mutual is not known, but a few hours after Dorsey had accosted him, Hooper rode Kit to water and never returned. Two days after he was ferried across the lower waters of the Guyandotte, seventy miles distant from the salt-works. The ferryman recognized him as one of the salt-works hands and asked him where he was bound.

"Up the country a piece. Why?" was Hooper's reply.

"Why, I don't know," said the ferryman, "why I asked the question, unless it was to learn if you had quit the salt-works."

Hooper made no further reply but paid the ferriage and ascended the hill on his journey.

It is a writer's privilege to digress and moralize at pleasure, and this right is not exercised with the view of advancing something better, but to furnish a resting place for the reader along a dreary stretch of monotony that wearies alike his eyes and mind. In this instance, we desire to direct attention to the workings of the inner man as he moves along in a strange country, a refugee from home and law.

As self-protection is the first law of nature, it is not surprising that ever since Hooper's leave of the boys at the board tree the thought of protection of self had been ever uppermost in his mind. But now, as the evening shades are falling, the man weary of a long ride, and feeling that he is beyond the reach of pursuit, approaches a farm whose surroundings generate thoughts in keeping with his already painful reflections. The farm lay to the right of the road he was traversing; upon the left were thick woods. Emerging from the latter were two or three little boys driving a yoke of oxen that were pulling a sled laden with fire-wood. Hooper sat still on his horse until they reached the road. During the brief interval a counterpart to this picture came vividly to his mind, softening his iron nature until he addressed them with fatherly recognition and tenderness. He was aroused from this delightful reverie of a moment to hear the cold reply to his tender speech in the rude question:

"Who are you?"

Hooper's rough exterior may have justified such an impertinent return for the strange familiarity with which he addressed these children.

There is more or less depravity in every nature, but so long as there can be found a tender chord in the heart which, when struck by memory's touch of old affection, will vibrate a tear or a sigh, then the depravity is not total. Hooper drew his handkerchief quickly across his eyes and sadly said:

"I forgot."

CHAPTER V. "Old Smith"

It will doubtless be of some interest to readers to know something of the efforts made by the friends of Stockstill and the legal authorities toward the apprehension of Hooper ere the excitement consequent upon the tragedy subsided. To this end we will return to John Hatfield who had attended the burial of his uncle's remains and returned home with a graphic description of Hooper and his horse. His information was imparted to his wife with measured precision. She listened with restrained impatience, and when he had finished said:

"That very same man came here the morning you left. I know it must be the same man, for that's just the way he looked, and that black mare and everything were just as you say. He came to the fence and called while I was dressing, and Bounce ran out and made such a noise that I went to the door and looked out, and saw him on the horse. He asked me who lived here. I told him, and then he asked if you were at home, and then I told him that you had gone to Uncle David's burial at McMinnville. He said he didn't know who Uncle David was. No, I reckon he didn't. He is the man who killed Uncle David, and if I'd a-known it, he'd never a-got away from this place. I wonder what a man could be doing riding 'round here so early and not get down, and not tell his business, but say he was lost."

"Did anyone besides yourself see him?"

"No, I was the only one up."

"Did you notice which way he went?"

"I think he went up the big road."

"Well, I'm just like you. I'll bet anything he is the identical bloody villain. The sheriff and posse have been searching about his home for him, but they are off the track. I will go to Sparta tomorrow and shall, perhaps, be able to get some clew to his course. What name did he leave?"

"He said his name was Smith."

The next day Hatfield met a lively party near the village of Sparta engaged in a shooting match. A turkey tied to a stump one hundred yards distant was the target. It required a good marksman and a good gun to win without several shots—the rule being to draw blood above the knees. As Hatfield rode up a man stepped forward and toed the mark, saying:

"Cl'ar the track youens, an' give 'Old Smith' a crack. I kinder think she'll fetch him!"

DOCK BROWN

All eyes were turned on the speaker. The report of the rifle was clear, and the gobbler fluttered and died amidst a general "Hurrah for 'Old Smith'!" The first shot had won.

The gun was then passed around. Dorsey was the marksman. Hatfield approached him, and the two men, at the request of the latter, stepped aside from the crowd, Dorsey wondering what the stranger could want with him. Hatfield made his business known in a few words.

"I am in pursuit of Gulliam Hopper," he said. "Whom I have reason to suspect has changed his name to Smith. I learn that he came this way."

"Came what way?"

"This way from McMinnville to Sparta. You have heard of the Stockstill murder?"

"No, I haven't."

Their conversation was interrupted by the appearance of the sheriff and others who had just arrived upon the ground. Their business was soon known to all, and Dorsey's gun and its name made a connecting link in the chain of pursuit, the plans of which were discussed during the remainder of the evening. It was finally agreed that Hatfield should return to McMinnville and inform the relatives and others that the sheriff was on the track and would go on to Loy's Cross Roads.

This news was gladly received by many, for it was well known that the sheriff was a veritable bloodhound when on the track of a man. "He has not failed yet and will not fail now," was the general sentiment. But the justice who issued the warrant was of a different opinion.

"They'll never catch Gulliam Hopper," he said. "I know him too well to believe that he will ever be arrested. I tell you he is no fool. Besides he is riding one of the fastest and best bottomed animals that ever made a mark on Tennessee soil. He not only has the advantage but he is stout, game, and doubtless well armed, and it would take a half dozen sheriffs to bring him here. He was hard to manage before this difficulty, and now, grown desperate, a small force had letter let him alone."

The pursuing party reached Loy's and there received information that a man answering to their description of Hopper had passed that way. But traveling on a few miles further, the trail grew cold, was lost, and finally abandoned.

Among the first to meet the sheriff on his return was Absalom

Hopper, who was ignorant of the direction his father had taken but now, learning that he had been seen at Sparta, had left his gun there, and that the sheriff was after him, he feared the result. Knowing the mettle of both sides, he believed that a meeting would be the death of somebody. But the sheriff returned empty-handed, and assured him that the pursuit was abandoned—that he was further behind, upon a more double track, at Loy's than at Sparta.

Absalom went to Sparta, saw Dorsey, bought his father's gun and brought it home.

CHAPTER VI. Mrs. Terrill

John Hooper rode away, leaving the boys, ox-team and sled in the road. The keen cracking of hickory whips and shrill notes of paw paw whistles grew faint and fainter in his ear. He leaned forward and half-consciously grasped the man in the hand which held the reins. What his thoughts were we may never know. Certainly they must have been bitter. The vision of home that had thus been conjured up by this chance meeting of children in the road, so swiftly followed by the reflections that he had forfeited all that made life desirable by the act of a moment of ungovernable passion, weighed heavily upon his heart and filled his heart with the gloom of despair.

It was dark when he reached the next farm-house, where he obtained food and lodging, which were tendered him with old-fashioned Virginia hospitality, free as its own mountain air.

The farmer with whom he stopped also kept a store of moderate capacity, yet sufficient to supply the surrounding conutry with nearly all the staple articles of domestic use. Coffee, calico, etc., were exchanged for jeans, linseys, etc., the products of the busy house-wives' looms.

Hooper bought a cottonade suit of his host and paid for it in work upon the farm. He looked more the impersonation of abject poverty than a man of money. Yet he had plenty of the latter for his purpose—far more than the generality of men in those days.

Better clad than usual, he dug up his specie—which he had buried as usual—mounted faithful Kit, and rode away for other parts.

He halted at a house on the banks of the great Kanawha, in a neighborhood now known as Hawk's Nest in the state of Virginia. The house was a neat double-log building, surrounded by a small farm, a little weather-beaten but in good condition.

His hail was kindly answered by a female who asked him to

alight. He did so, and obtained permission to spend the night. His hostess was a widow, the mother of one child, a son of seventeen, whom she designated as Jimmy. Supper over, Hopper sat and conversed with the two, of the late spring, high water, and himself. She talked little, yet was evidently pleased with the compliments the stranger paid herself and her home. Having acquainted himself with her widowhood and loneliness and told her that his name was Hooper, and that he was from north Kentucky; that he once had a large family, but all were dead; that tired of the land in which all that made life dear had perished, he was then seeking a home in Virginia; that he preferred farming, provided that he could get a place to suit him—a place he could look upon as really his home; that he was weary of traveling, and in conclusion asked her if she knew of a place that she thought would suit him.

"No," she said, "I don't. I've got no neighbors hardly, and don't know nothin' 'bout people 'round here."

This was a cooler answer than Hooper had expected, for he had begun to flatter himself with the belief that he was gaining her favor. But he made the best of it by changing the subject. A few more compliments he ventured, and was then shown to his room. When Jimmy left him to himself, he pulled in the latch-string and retired to bed. Next morning he felt greatly refreshed from a good night's rest.

Everything about the place bore the marks of neatness, and if he came to the breakfast table with smiling face and carefully combed and parted hair, he should by no means be the subject of censure at the hands of those who are poorer judges of women's nature than he. He was only fifty-four and in full vigor of mind and body. Besides, a man seldom loses, if he has ever possessed it, appreciation for order, neatness, or beauty, or other attractive qualities so often perfected in the gentler sex.

Hooper, though unpolished himself, made a discovery of the two former qualities, at least in his hostess, and admired them the more because they seemed innate. The floors, the counterpanes, the old furniture, the mantels, were not clean and orderly merely for show, for she had no visitors, but because such was the widow's preference.

Mrs. Terrell (for that was her name) would not allow her guest to depart without an effort to disclose a weakness she had already begun to feel for him. It was done through the channel of sympathy. She said:

Outlaw of Grayson County

"I am alone in the world. I haven't got no relations in natur' that I know of 'cept Jim. I wasn't grown when I run off with my husband. It was because the old folks opposed it. We come all the way from Pennsylvania here, and never went back. They're all dead now—Mr. Terrell and all my children, 'cept Jim. You can see out yander where they're buried." And she pointed to a few cedars that sheltered four graves, enclosed with a rail fence, in the stalkfield. There slept the husband, two daughters and one son.

Hooper was deeply touched. Those of whom he had not heard for a year came to his mind, but he nerved himself at the thought of the widow's situation, regarded the occasion as his opportunity, and remarked that inasmuch as his horse was not fully rested, he would if she did not object, remain another night. She consented. He stopped that night, and another. Evincing a genuine sympathy, he was soon ingratiated into her affections, and permitted to make her house his home. The Terrell farm soon wore a lively and prosperous appearance under Hooper's and Jimmy's control.

A year passed, and few persons saw Hooper. He kept close at home. Jimmy did the errands, while Hooper was the master-spirit of the place. They prospered and seemed happy until the fall of eighteen hundred and thirty-one when Jimmy was taken ill. A physician was summoned, but too late; the boy was fast sinking, and in a few days passed beyond mortal aid. Three or four neighbors assisted in laying him with the family dead among the cedars.

There was some gossip among the females of the scant and scattered neighborhood concerning the manner in which Hooper and Mrs. Terrell were living. Some declared their husbands ought to drive such people from the country. Others said, "Hang her!" Still others, "Burn her!" Always accompanying these words and others of like impress with abusive epithets, such as have been common, either in thought or expression from the time Eve dreamed a bee flew out and stung her to the present. What is, and what has been, the cause of this murderous feeling in the breast of the woman toward the unfortunate of her sex, from Mrs. Noah to Mrs. Brigham Young? Is the impulse hell-born or divine? It may be the latter, and as natural and as deeply ingrained as the principle of love—their natures for the weal of humanity—for the elevation, preservation, and purification of a higher standard of purity and holiness in our race. Let it come from what source it may, it is as often found in the realms of virtue as in the purlieus of vice.

But Hooper and the widow heeded not what little they heard of the gossip that went on about them. They moved along their daily walk, feeling, like most newly married people do, that they didn't lack many of being all the important personages in the world; yet they knew by that mysterious intuition under which such circumstances ever are the monitor of a guilty conscience, that they were the subject of considerable plain talk. This knowledge generated extra selfishness and seclusion. Few came to see them, and the greater number of these were detached portions of Mrs. Grundy's retinue, actuated by prurient curiosity, and hopeful of gathering fresh food for scandal.

If the proposition, "Human nature is the same the world over," be true, then a similarity of circumstances in individual instances will generate a recognizable affinity between them.

Hooper and Mrs. Terrell had become familiar with each other's antecedents—at least to the extent that they were far from old loved spots, friends and familiar faces—unpopular strangers in a hostile community. Thus they were drawn nearer together, and each leaned on the other for comfort and strength. They entertained a reciprocal regard, an attachment growing out of mutual independence rather than affection,. which latter is always based upon genuine or imaginary merit.

Since Jimmy's death, the extra duties imposed upon Hooper brought him in occasional contact with people of the county seat. After making the acquaintance of most persons of the neighborhood he gradually grew more reconciled with his lot and felt more secure from apprehension. He learned to refer to Mrs. Terrell's property as his own, and she, yielding to his every wish, regarded him not only as her best friend but as her husband.

CHAPTER VII. Harry Skelton

Harry Skelton was a law student at McMinnville and was on the eve of entering the profession at the time of the Stockstill tragedy. He was reared upon a farm, but his education had not been neglected. His stature was six feet, his form well proportioned, his features regular and handsome, and the expression of his countenance bright and intelligent. When a boy, in the discussions of the "debating society" that was ever the penchant of country schools in those days, he proved himself possessed of unusual natural polemic powers, and displayed wonderful command of language and graces of oratory. The universal prediction of his friends was, "He'll make his mark in the world."

Flattery proves to be in tar too many instances a keen and deadly dagger thrust into the vitals of young and precocious youth. Fortunately, Skelton proved to be an exception to this rule. He possessed brain as well as talent and was wise beyond his years. He well knew that intellectual greatness, as well as physical triumphs, could only be attained by and through untiring effort.

McMinnville and its neighborhood having been his home from his earliest infancy, he felt that he could make more rapid advancement in his profession among strangers, and consequently, in the year eighteen hundred and thirty-one, he removed to Cannelton, Virginia, the shiretown of Fayette County, only twelve miles from Hopper's new home. It was not long before he established a reputation not only as an able advocate but as a lawyer of industry, erudition and trustworthiness. Such was his candor and fairness in argument that he soon won the confidence of the people to the extent that when he stated a proposition as law, juries unhesitatingly accepted it as true. There were older and better lawyers in the town, but they all entertained great respect for Skelton's legal opinions.

One cold January morning of eighteen hundred and thirty-three, whilst Skelton was seated by his office fire, intently engaged in reading a law book open before him, a figure darkened the door.

"Walk in, sir, walk in and have a chair," said the young lawyer. "Cold morning, this."

"Well," rejoined the intruder, "not so cold as you might suppose. I'm a little hot myself. Reckon I look so, too?"

Skelton looked up at his visitor's face. One eye was nearly closed, the effect of a blow, and his countenance was considerably bruised and scratched.

"Well, yes," said Skelton, "you look a little like you had been in harness. Got the worst of it, I guess?"

"No, I'll be damned if I did, either. If I know anything about it, I give him a floggin', an' if they'd let me alone I'd a-killed him. But what I came here for is to see you about it. You're a lawyer, I s'pose, an' I reckon I hev to hire you. Do you think you can get me clean outen the scrape? How much you goin' to charge me?"

"That I don't know, sir, until I learn something of the facts connected with the case. It may be that you will not need a lawyer."

"Yes, but I do. I've got to hev a lawyer, for they're goin' to hev me up."

"State your case then, and I'll tell you what I can perhaps do for you."

"Well," said the visitor, "about an hour ago—or, s'posin' you was not to blame, now; that you was goin' 'long 'tending to your own business, an' he'd a-come up an' begun the thing with you, he'd a-raised the fuss hisself, what'd be the law in that case?" The man hitched his chair close to the lawyer and asked the question in a tone that indicated he would not put up with an answer unfavorable to his side.

Skelton suppressed a strong inclination to laugh, but feeling that a chance for a fee was at stake, and, with a face as serious as his interlocutor's, replied that it depended in a great deal on what the thing was the other party had begun, and what his prospective client did in reprisal, and that if he only knew all the facts and circumstances of the case he would then be able to apply the law.

"Then, s'posin' this, now——"

"Hold a moment," said Skelton. "My dear sir, please tell the facts as they are in the whole case—the names of the parties, what they did, how the difficulty began, progressed, and ended, and leave out all this 's'posin' ' for I must know everything if I am to undertake your defense."

"Then, ef you must know, I'll tell you. I come to mill yestiddy, an' hed to stay all night afore I could git my grindin'. This mornin' was so col' that I thought I'd take sumthin' to warm me up. I went in the grocery and got a drink, an' then sot down by the fire. There was sev'ral in the house an' saw the whole thing from fust to last, an' they all know 'xac'ly how it was. Well, Sam Duncan he comes up to me an' says, says he, 'You're this Terrell man, I b'lieve.' Says I, 'Thet's not my name.' He says that it didn't make no difference ef it wasn't my name, that I was the Terrell man anyhow, an' if I didn't like it I could lump it. I tol' him he had better

Outlaw of Grayson County

'ten' to his own business an' let mine alone. He says he was able to 'ten' to his own business an' mine too, thet I ought to be whipt, an' he was the chap that could do it. He says something else then, an' I struck him, an' we went at it. Now, kin you get me out?"

"Did you hurt him much?"

"I kinder think so. I bit his ear off, an'———"

"Goodness! My friend, you are in a bad fix. You are guilty of mayhem, a felony punished by confinement in the penitentiary. No, let me see, I am mistaken. It is not mayhem. But had it been a finger or eye——."

"I took his eye out but it went back. What'll you charge to git me out?"

"Have you been arrested?"

"No."

"Have you any one here to go upon your bond?"

"What bond?"

"A bond for your appearance at the trial."

"O, there's no need of no bond for thet, I'll be on han' then."

"Yes, but it is the duty of the officer to arrest you and detain you in custody, or send you to jail until the day of trial, unless some responsible person will enter into bond with you for your appearance. If this be done, you can go home and stay until the day of trial."

"I don't know whether I kin git anybody or not. Won't you go on it? I'll be here cert'n."

"Yes, if you can't get anyone else, and they will accept me. Now about the fee."

"Yes, thet is what I was thinkin' 'bout. What are you goin' to charge me, and inshore me to get cl'ar?"

"I will not take the case by insurance, but I will defend you the best I can for fifteen dollars cash."

"Whew! Why, man, it'd break me up. I couldn't make thet much in three weeks. An' here you are wantin' to charge me thet jest to git up an' tell a few lies an' 'buse t' other fellow. F-i-f-t-e-e-n d-o-l-l-a-r-s! No, sir, I can't git it. I'd ruther let 'em do what they can with me than to pay a jackleg lawyer thet much. They shorely can't do eny worse than thet, kin they?"

"You are to be your own judge about that. And let me tell you this: If you think lawyers are paid fees for telling lies and abusing the opposing side, you have applied to the wrong man. I will have nothing further to say to you about the case. But I wish to say this—that you are like some other people in this country, who seem to have come to the conclusion that lawyer is a synonym for general rascality; that the profession is only a medium through which the spite and malice existing between neighbors are to find expression. Whether your opinion is a general one or not, I don't know, but I shall not consider that you have special reference to me."

"O, no. Can't you take a joke?"

"Certainly I can, when a man is joking. But I tell you the people are generally mistaken in this matter. The profession of law is an honorable one. It is a necessary one. True, there are bad men in every business of life. Yet the man who is so uncharitable as to censure the whole for the faults of a few, in my opinion, belongs to the latter class, and holds a very prominent position there. I am satisfied that one great reason why professional men, especially lawyers, are so abused, and often so unpopular, is because of the public nature of their business. Almost every species and kind of sentiment that may entertain in time finds expressions. Like all humanity, they are sometimes in ill humor, and whilst in that frame say things in their argument, and sometimes do things in the management of their cases, that are wrong. And this is not always the result of ill humor, but of ambition, a desire to succeed, to excel. Farmers and others are subjected to such trials. Neither does their business expose to public scrutiny their every act and transaction. Let them be turned inside out to the public gaze as are lawyers, and———."

The constable at this moment appeared at the door with a strip of paper in his hand.

"Come in!" said Mr. Skelton.

The officer entered and spoke to Hooper, who seemed somewhat agitated, and informed him of the fact that he was an officer of the law and had a warrant for his arrest. He then read the charge, which was assault and battery, told the accused that his trial would be on the following Monday, and then asked Hooper to accompany him.

"Where to?" asked Hooper.

"To the Squire's office," said the officer.

"What for?"

"Why, either to give bond or be sent to jail. If you can furnish surety in the sum of fifty dollars, you can go home, otherwise to jail."

"Go to jail! There ain't enough men in Cannelton to take me to jail! Do you s'pose I'm to be run over like a hound, let a man abuse me like a dog, an' let me say nothin' to him? No, sir, I'll not do it. I'll die first!"

"I've nothing to do with that. I have a duty to perform, and I am not going to shrink from it. If you have done nothing wrong, you are likely to come out all right. But you see Duncan's ear is nearly bitten off, and it is thought he will lose one of his eyes. I know nothing, however, of the case. Come along with me."

"Hold a moment," said Skelton. "I stand good for him." He wrote the requisite bond, signed it, and handed it to the officer who expressed himself as satisfied and withdrew.

CHAPTER VIII.   The Trial—Recognition

A throng of country people assembled in town on the day of trial. Hooper was there early in the morning. His witnesses had been summoned and were in attendance. Skelton had conversed with them and discovered that facts were rather more favorable to Hooper than he had at first been led to suppose by the latter's rambling disconnected version of the affray. Yet he was satisfied a breach of peace had been made by his client; but, not unlike most lawyers, he had concluded that his client should be acquitted. This belief, although often the cause of much censure upon the part of the populace, is nevertheless one which is necessary for the advocate to entertain, at least during the progress of the trial, in order to call into action the most brilliant efforts of native eloquence and ingenuity. It is unquestionably true that such belief sometimes greatly conduces to the exercise of over-zeal in the defense of a poor criminal; yet, if restrained within the bounds of an honorable discharge of duty, the attorney will not be punished for it either here below or in the court above. A fellow-feeling akin to brotherly love is aroused in the breast of a lawyer as soon as the relation of attorney and client is established. It is a mingled feeling of pride, sympathy and protection. Pride, that he is the one chosen to defend; sympathy, that he is in confidence and has been entrusted with the secrets of the case; protection, that the client is greatly dependent upon his exertions for a successful issue from the ordeal.

The hour for trial arrived. The court room was crowded when the constable stepped to the door and cried, "Hear ye, Hear ye! etc."

Sam Duncan had sufficiently recovered from his injuries to appear as the chief witness for the prosecution. His eye, not lost, was closed and covered. From his injured optic he cast a glance of defiance at his adversary which was met with an overmatch from the vindictive eyes of Hooper. These defiant glances and whispered threats and occasional scowls were detected and summarily suppressed by a few sharp, incisive words from the court. The counsel for the prosecution announced his readiness to proceed to trial.

"Are you ready, Mr. Skelton?" asked the justice.

"Presently, your honor," said Skelton who was conferring with his client.

"We will try," he continued a moment later.

"Call up the jury, Mr. Constable," said the court to that official.

The jury was duly empaneled, and Sam Duncan was put on the witness stand. He was taller than the ordinary run of men, rawboned in appearance, and gave token of great physical strength. A carpenter by trade, he made a good living from his occupation, but would often indulge in "big sprees," and expend all the money he had on hand. During these spells of debauchery he frequently got into fights, but had never before encouraged a John Hooper. He was designated "The Bull of Fayette." When he emerged from the encounter with Hooper, his surprise at his discomfiture was fully equal to the physical pain he was compelled to endure, and his signal defeat was the source of some pleasure to the citizens, and especially to those who had been the victims of his ungovernable temper and fistic prowess.

That it is a disgrace to be feared by one's neighbors is certainly true. There are men in almost every community who pride themselves upon their muscular development and their reputation for using their strength to the bodily hurt of their fellowmen. Such characters always receive the outward show of friendly greeting, while in the hearts of every one they are feared and detested, and, as in the case of Duncan, when they meet a master and are severely punished, a private chuckle of satisfaction pervades the entire community.

Duncan's statements to the jury were as true, doubtless, as he could recollect. They were corroborated in their main points—except that he was making no demonstration to fight Hooper at the time he insulted the latter—by succeeding witnesses, all of whom concurred in the statement of an important fact which had probably escaped Duncan's memory, to-wit: that he had forced the difficulty upon his adversary.

The evidence was concluded, Skelton arose and asked the court to instruct the jury if they believed from the testimony that Hooper had reasonable grounds for believing, and did believe, that

Outlaw of Grayson County

unless prevented Duncan would strike him, they must find for the defendant, unless they should also believe that the defendant used more force than was necessary to repel the attack.

This instruction was given with but little modification. Skelton then began his speech by saying that his client was guilty of no offense under the charge; that there was no law known to civilization which deprived a man of the right of self-protection. Concluding, he said: "If a man is in the wrong at the beginning he can not get right during the progress of a difficulty. You all know Sam Duncan. You know, too, that if Hooper needed chastisement for the manner in which he lives with Mrs. Terrell, Sam should be the last man to mete it out to him. That his language was very unbecoming and insulting, and that he made threatening advances, no one of you can doubt."

At this point the speaker's glance fell full upon the eyes of his client. He paused a moment; his cheeks blanched and his frame trembled. The constable and others ran to him and asked if he were ill, and if so, tendered their services in any manner he might require. After drinking a glass of water some thoughtful person handed him, he resumed his speech, with an apology for what occurred, saying that he was overcome by the sudden recollection of a terrible affair he had witnessed some years before and wherein his own life was greatly endangered. He would probably explain on some other occasion.

"If Hopper—Hooper, I mean—is not living as he should," he continued, "the law may handle him, but an individual has not that right, and the law should punish one who thus takes it in hand." Immediately after concluding his speech, Skelton left the court room and hurriedly repaired to his office.

The prosecutor's speech was brief and pointed. He told the jury that it was evident that the law had been violated, the public peace infracted; that Duncan was not in the right was true enough, but neither was Hooper right—they both were wrong. But they were not now trying Duncan; his case would come up thereafter. Asking the jury to inflict a fine upon the defendant, he concluded by expressing his sympathy for the strange and sudden illness of Mr. Skelton, and declaring that it would be unjust to the latter for him to make a lengthy argument in his absence from the court room, therefore he would submit the case as it then stood. The jury retired and after brief deliberation returned and rendered a verdict of "not guilty."

Skelton's "break-down"—as the crowd termed it—in his speech

was as unaccountable to Hooper as it was to the other spectators. He little imagined that in the sparkle of his eyes as they met his attorney's gaze there was anything to remind the other of the murder of Stockstill. He totally failed to recognize Skelton, and did not dream that he was the youth who had fled in terror from him on that fateful day in the Tennessee forest. He knew him but slightly as a boy, and the man had grown beyond his knowledge. Skelton had changed much; Hooper but little. Besides, boys remember men better than men can remember boys.

By the time the jury returned with their verdict Skelton had returned to the court room. He and Hooper then together repaired to his office. They had agreed upon the fee of fifteen dollars previous to the trial. Hooper unhesitatingly paid the money, saying: "I was sorry you broke down so. What was the matter with you anyhow?"

"I dislike to explain," said Skelton, "but it is due you that I should. And what I shall say will not be intended to wound your feelings. I think I have seen you before, and cannot help believing your real name is Hopper."

"Pshaw! feller, what makes you think thet? An' ef it was—which it aren't—what's thet to make you sick?"

"If you will promise not to get enraged I will tell you."

"Of course, I won't get mad," said Hooper, but there was a suspicious huskiness in his voice as he spoke.

"Well," said Skelton, "did you ever know David Stockstill, of Tennessee?"

There it was at last. His crime, in this out-of-the-way region where he had all these years imagined himself secure from detection, confronted him. He knew that he was recognized. He had but two courses to pursue to secure immunity from denunciation, perhaps arrest. If he could make Skelton believe it was a case of mistaken identity, the result of an accidental resemblance between him and the person the lawyer took him to be, the other contingency need not present itself.

Partially put on his guard by Skelton's assertion that he believed him to be Hopper, he had no time to gain full command of all his faculties before the question, "Did you know David Stockstill?" came full upon him.

He reddened, hesitated a second, and then answered in a choking manner and rasping tone, "No sir, I never did."

But this time, moved by nervous excitement superinduced by the dramatic situation, both men had arisen to their feet. Skelton, well knowing his man, feared serious trouble. Hooper, knowing that he

Outlaw of Grayson County

was discovered, was anxious to get away from his lawyer's presence. Yet there was an evil, devilish expression on the man's face that foreboded mischief, which Skelton was not slow to discover, and to parry any ill design that might be forming in the former's breast, he hastened to stammer an apology.

"What do you mean?" gasped Hooper.

Skelton, from the beginning of the conversation, had kept his hand in his pant's pocket, firmly clutching the handle of one of those new instruments of destruction recently invented by Col. Sam Colt and now obsolete but remembered as the "pepperbox" revolver. He knew that he had invaded the domain of danger the moment he gave token of having recognized Hooper. He now discovered impatient desperation in the tone of this last question, but as quietly and coolly as possible replied:

"Nothing in particular, only I thought I had seen you before in Tennessee. I never meant to offend you."

Hooper approached the door, took hold of the handle and was in the act of closing it, when Skelton excitedly exclaimed. "Don't you do that! The door must remain open, sir!"

"Well, now, here, you need'nt be feared of me. I'm not goin' to hurt you, but I do want you to tell me why you thought you'd seen me afore, an' how you happened to think of it while you were speakin'. You was in this office with me afore thet, an' never said a word about it."

Skelton knew that he was not mistaken in the man, but he had ventured into an awkward predicament—a decidedly unpleasant situation—from which it was now his intention to extricate himself in the best manner possible. He felt himself cornered. Serious questions were being put to him by a man whom he knew to be a moral wreck, who regarded neither his own life nor that of another. The fire of his eyes indicated a murderous heart. He once thought it would be best to leave the office, denounce Hooper to the authorities, and procure his arrest; but upon reflection concluded that it would be wrong inasmuch as the man was his client and he had made the discovery during relationship. Besides, several years had passed since the killing of Stockstill, and as far as he was concerned the matter should rest for the present at least. To himself he said, "If I can induce him to believe that I am now convinced that I was mistaken, I will do so."

"I am sorry, Mr. Hopper—Hooper, I mean—that a singular course of my imagination has excited such a strange curiosity. In my own thoughts it is possible that I have done you a very great injustice.

I would be glad of your assurance that this apology is sufficient to satisfy you of my mistake, without further explanation which could not be given without reference to a terrible affair of the past, the very thought of which I would gladly erase from my memory." He then waved his hand, indicating a desire to drop the subject.

But Hooper was not willing to drop it. Said he, "I don't like to bother you. I know you never seen me afore in your life, but then you've got my curiosity up, an' I want to know what it is thet's so awful to you. Tell me, now, an' I won't say nothin' more about it."

Finding that he could not get off otherwise than by a full disclosure, Skelton said: "Some five or six years ago, in Warren County, Tennessee, near McMinnville, I saw a man named Gulliam Hooper—Hopper—I beg your pardon again—I saw Gulliam Hopper shoot and kill David Stockstill, and then he attempted to kill me, and would have done so, no doubt, had I not run away. The look he gave me I shall never forget. I won't mean any harm when I say that you and Hopper bear a striking resemblance to each other. At least, when I turned to you during my speech I discovered an excited gleam in your eyes which reminded me of his on the occasion to which I refer. I had learned how long you had been in this county from the evidence, and by the association of ideas, in connection with a look which I thought I recognized, all in a flash, I thought I was positive that you were Hopper. But understand me now, I am perfectly satisfied with your assurance to the contrary and am truly sorry if I have hurt your feelings."

"O, thet's all right," said Hooper. "I am glad thet you don't think thet I'm thet man. I don't know nothin' in the world about thet. I'm from Kentucky, an' don't know anybody in Tennessee. An' as no harm's done it's all right, an' I'll go home."

To Skelton's relief, he then took his departure.

CHAPTER IX. Mr. and Mrs. John Brown

Mrs. Terrell had been quite uneasy about the probable result of the trial, for Hopper was all on earth to her. She was therefore greatly relieved, as well as pleased, when the joyous barking of the dog announced his arrival at the gate long after dark, and she learned of his acquittal.

Good, strong coffee, a warm hoe-cake and nicely broiled ham were kept ready for him, and the anxious woman was pained to observe that he did not relish them with his usual hearty appetite. She inquired if he were sick.

"No, I'm not sick," was his reply, "but I'm in a heap o' trouble."

"What on earth?" she asked.

"O, don't bother me now. It's nothing that concerns you. Go to bed and let me alone," was the surly answer she received.

Mrs. Terrell had grown accustomed to his occasional rough and unkind words, and when he was in such a mood would most generally let him alone; but tonight it was with great reluctance that she yielded him obedience.

The morning came. Breakfast was over. A heavy fall of snow whitened air and earth. A more cheerless morning could not well be conceived. Hooper sat by the blazing hearth with his elbows on his knees and his face in his hands, lost in thought.

Mrs. Terrell came to him and, placing a hand upon his shoulder, said: "Do tell me now what is the matter. What has gone wrong with you?"

"I can't tell you all," he said, "but I've got to leave you. I must leave these diggin's. It's no use for you to cry an' take on about it. I'm boun' to go. I must, I MUST!"

"Then, may I go with you?"

"No, ma'am, it wouldn't do now. Nobody must know whar I'm goin' to."

"O, I can never stand this," cried the poor woman. "Do tell me what you have to leave for, an' let me go with you. Just think o' my bein' left here alone, an' never to see you ag'in. Ef you thought anything of me you'd tell me all about your troubles an' take me with you."

"Well, ma'am," he replied, "I killed a man in Tennessee several years ago, an' run away. I come here, an' now it's about to be found out on me. I was talkin' to a feller yestiddy who saw me shoot the man. He said he knew me, but I think I almost made him believe he didn't. But I am afeard he'll find me out, an' then you know what they'd do with me. Ef you want to go with me now, after what I've told you, then I'll take you."

"Indeed, I'll go. I'd go with you to the end of the world, no matter what you've done," was the woman-like response.

"Then you'll hev to sell out, an' it must be done soon. I don't know of but one man who'd buy the place."

"No, no!" exclaimed Mrs. Terrell, "we must not sell the place. I'm a poor, wretched woman. I'm bad, I know, but I love my dear old home, an' I can't sell the dear ashes of my chilluns. You know Jimmy's over thar, an' you loved him. I'll go away from the place, but I'll never sell it. We may want to come back to it ag'in some day. Anyhow, I want to be buried over thar in the field, no matter whar I die."

"Then we'll not fuss about it. We'll only sell the stock, all 'cept Kit and Roan, an' the go-cart. We'll need 'em, you know, to travel with. An' while I think of it, there is another thing to be done. We must change our names. You'll be my wife, an' I'll be John Brown."

That evening John Hooper went over to see a neighbor who had expressed a desire for the place and purchase of furniture, stock, etc., were soon made and accepted. This neighbor had recently come to the vicinity from northern Virginia, and was extremely anxious to settle there. The rent price for the farm was agreed upon at one-fourth of the whole crop raised. The price of the livestock, furniture, etc., was paid cash in hand. Hooper told him they were going to New York, and would let him hear from them in due time relative to the rent.

The go-cart was exchanged for a small box-bed wagon, in which provisions for the journey were stored. Mrs. Terrell seemed satisfied with the disposition of the property, but frequently expressed a desire to know their destination. Hooper assured her that she should know in good time—that it was not best to tell her now. As every hour of delay in preparation for the journey was one of almost unbearable suspense for Hooper, they were not long in getting ready.

It was about the first of March when old Kit and Roan were harnessed, and Mr. and Mrs. John Brown were climbing the snowy hills to the westward, their destination being the mouth of Big Sandy. It was one hundred miles from Cannelton to the confluence of the Ohio and Big Sandy rivers, but Brown and his wife (?) reached the vicinity after five days' travel over a rough and broken country.

It required no small effort on the part of Mrs. Brown to remember her new name. On one occasion, whilst at the supper table, during their journey, she addressed her husband as Mr. Hooper. They had previously given their names as Brown and had their lapsus lingue been discovered by the family, her embarrassment would have proved to their entertainers that they were traveling under an assumed name. For this "slip of the tongue," when they were alone, Brown abused the poor woman with heartless severity.

To say that it is neither safe nor right to burden a woman's mind and conscience with important secrets when it can be avoided should not be construed as unjust to her. It is not right, because it renders her unhappy. It is not safe, because she will at some time innocently betray. It bears upon her mind with the weight of a self-guilty thought and single idea. Hence the disclosure. The exquisitely-fine composition of her whole being, with its delicate texture of tender sensibilities, is too weak for the safe harboring of such bulky prisoners. Man is of rougher and sterner stuff. The ills imposed upon our race by the ordinary vicissitudes of life are borne with apparently greater ease by woman, yet it is for this reason that her fortitude exceeds her ability, while man's ability exceeds his fortitude.

When Brown arrived at Catlettsburg, near the mouth of the river, he had about eight hundred dollars in specie. After a careful reconnaissance of the premises, he deposited in the earth all but fifty dollars. A week after, he rented and settled in a little cabin on the banks of the Big Sandy, about a mile from the town. He supplied several families in the place with firewood and was thus enabled to earn a livelihood without being compelled to draw upon his hidden store. He also procured a trot-line and engaged in the fishing business. In this he was quite successful and sold more fish than the regular fishermen of the port. The usual rivalry, however, sprang up between them, the same as that we discover today in every trade and profession in life.

Brown's character, to some extent, had changed. The disposition to face, rather than avoid, a difficulty, so prominent in Hopper, Hooper, etc., was reversed in the person of John Brown. We do not wish to convey the idea that he had become a coward, for that would be erroneous. Had he been attacked, he would have fought with the old fury and bravery. But he had not now the same willingness to resent an insult that had hitherto characterized his intercourse with the world. So, when Old Rufus, the fisherman, accused him of stealing fish from his box, he only gave it the lie and passed on about his business. The man who is led and controlled by his angry passions, lives fast and will soon "give over."

CHAPTER X. The Three Brothers

James, Pinkney, and Gulliam, it will be remembered, were three of the sons of Hopper. We do not deem it necessary, or even proper, to inquire into the character sustained by these young men during their stay at the old homestead in Tennessee, in the interim between the flight of their father and the period when the march of events brings them once more to our notice.

Having learned that their father had been seen at the salt-works a few years before, in the year of 1833—considering themselves free men, although James was the only one of the trio who had attained his majority—they turned their backs upon their home and their faces in the direction of Virginia, and started in search of their fugitive parent. They reached the salt-works and, without disclosing their names, learned that a man named Hooper, the description of whom at once established his identity in their minds, had been there and remained nearly a year, but he had departed mysteriously, and no tiding of him had since reached the works.

The boys left for the interior of the state, and settled temporarily at Calhoun, now in central West Virginia. Here they engaged in horse-swapping, cattle-buying and stock-trading. They would make occasional trips to Pennsylvania, Ohio and Kentucky. They were neat in their dress, rather reckless in their bearing, and were considered fast men in their day. James was about six feet in height, compactly built, inclined to stoutness, and weighed two hundred pounds. Pinkney was not so tall as his brother, boasted a well-proportioned form, with a mouth rather sharp and pointed, but withal presented a striking, if not handsome, appearance, that always attracted attention. Gulliam was a low, heavy-built man, dark-skinned, dark-haired, and with gray, or rather, wolf-eyes. A fuller description of their characters, and a ventilation of their operations not only in Virginia but elsewhere, will appear in the course of this narrative.

Passing over two or three years which they spent trading and traveling about the country, we find these young men one bright morning, enjoying a leisurely stroll along the banks of the Big Sandy, in the vicinity of Catlettsburg, where they had passed the previous night.

Having heard nothing of their father since leaving the salt-works, they had long ago arrived at the conclusion that he was dead.

Their attention was attracted by a man in a light canoe, running his trot-line far out in the river.

"Look what a large one!" exclaimed Gulliam. He'll not manage that cat. It'll turn him sure. There! Out he goes, by———! Just as I was going to say."

Sure enough, the fish gave a tremendous flounce, and the man was jerked overboard. He scrambled up, however, and caught the upset canoe. There was loud laughter and hearty cheering on the bank as the old man, pushing the boat before him, swam ashore. The boys went down to the water and spoke to him, but he was too much exhausted to reply, besides, he had heard the loud laughing, which he did not appreciate. Facing the river, he sat with cable in hand, disdaining the presence of the impertinent strangers.

The boys, tiring of his sulkiness, started off up the bank again, one of them saying, "Well, it is only fisherman's luck, old man, and you ought to be glad that you didn't drown. But, say, what become of your big fish?"

"O, he's thar, an' I'll git him yit." Saying this, the old man, for the first time, turned and faced the three young men.

A moment of absolute silence fell between them as they stood face to face. It was broken by James who suddenly inquired:

"What is your name, old man?"

"Brown, sir."

"I am sure," continued James, addressing his brothers, "it is father." Then turning to the old man again, "Don't you know me, father, your son, James? And here is Pink and Gulliam."

The old man's emotions proved too great for his years and strength, and he sank to the ground, sobbing and laughing hysterically in the midst of tears.

They told him of their long and fruitless search for him, and of the great change in his personal appearance since they last saw him.

"Yes, yes," said the old man, "I remember the last time, an' I know I've changed a good deal. I'm gittin' old. How's all at home? Does anybody know whar I am?"

"Nobody but us, that we know of."

"When did you leave home?"

"O, it's been a long time, but we hear from there every once in a while. They are all well. Where do you live, father?"

"In yan little house up thar," he replied, pointing to the cabin. "I go by the name o' Brown now. I've got a 'oman keepin' house fer me. Nobody here don't know my name, an' I tell 'em it's Brown, an' thet the 'oman is my wife."

"Who is she?" asked James.

"Well, thet don't make no difference now. I brung her here with me a long time ago. Whar did ye all come from? An' how did ye happen to come across me?"

"We didn't know you were in the land of living but supposed you dead. We hadn't heard from you since you left the salt-works."

"I spect we had better go to the house, boys, an' see the ole 'oman, an' tell her 'bout it an' let her see you. I reckon you are goin' to stay wi' me awhile, ain't you?"

They ascended the hill to the cabin. Mrs. Brown was greatly frightened at seeing them, for, as it was an unusual thing to see Brown with company, she very naturally jumped to the conclusion that he was under arrest. She was soon relieved of her groundless fears by an introduction to the young men. They had been in the house but a short time when Mr. Brown asked them to walk out with him. They entered the woods nearby and seated themselves upon the trunk of a fallen tree. The old man asked them many questions about the old home and the family, all of which were readily answered. None except the family had heard from them since they left home, and they had not written home for several weeks, but were expecting a letter from Moses, as they had requested him to write them at that place; that they had not been to the post office but were going that morning.

"I wish one o' you would go now. Gullie, you go, an' come back as quick as you kin. But be mighty keerful 'bout talkin' to folks. Ef ennybody axes you who you ar' tell 'em it's none o' their business. Run, now, an' hurry back."

During Gulliam's absence, the party discussed plans for future operations and safety. The first proposition came from James, and related to the disposal of Mrs. Brown, who, he said, was evidently in the way.

"What kin we do wi' her?" asked the old man.

"Why, damn it, we can pitch her in the river if nothing else will do," was the heartless reply.

"Hold on!" exclaimed Mr. Brown. "Now thet's goin' a leetle too fur. She's a pore helpless thing, an' has got no friends but me. She's been mighty good to me, an' I'm not agoin' to treat her in enny sich a bad way as thet. I'm boun' to hev her, ennyhow, to keep house for me."

"O, if you like her and need her; of course, if she never tells anything."

"She kin keep a secret as well as enny of us. But yander comes Gullie, an' I wonder if he's got a letter for us?"

Outlaw of Grayson County

As soon as the boy entered the skirt of woods, he drew a letter from his pocket and waved it up and down. They hurried to meet him, and breaking the seal, read:

McMinnville, Tenn.
March 10, 1835

Dear Brothers:

I take my pen in hand to drop you a few lines to let you know that we are all well, and I hope that when these few lines come to hand they will find you enjoying the same blessing. Your letter came safe to hand last month, and we was all glad to hear from you, but was sorry you had not heard from pap. I suppose he is dead. Nobody has broke open any of your letters yet, and I don't think they'll do so. If anybody does, they'll never break open another one. Mother is sorter getting over the trouble, but she says she thinks Gullie ought to come back and stay with her, and I think so, too. A great many of the boys 'round here keeps asking me where you are, but I tell them I don't know. If ever you find pap, or hear anything of him, you must write me about it. We are all fixing for a big crop. I'm going to put in some tobacco. I don't know what else to write, so I will bring my letter to a close, and say, write to me soon. Your brother till death,

Moses Hopper.

The old man took the half-sheet and stared at the writing. "Ah!" said he, "ef I could only go back—and—see!" He pressed his hands to his forehead and turned away.

"No, no, no!" cried the old man. "I'll never see 'em agin."

"Come, now," said James, "don't talk that way. Tell us what has become of Kit. Is she living?"

"Yes, she's up yander in the stable. She's got a colt, the finest black feller you ever seed. Want to go see him?"

Pinkney claimed the colt as soon as he clapped his eyes on him. And he really appeared so fond of him that his father told him that he should have him.

"Whar's your hosses?" asked the old man.

"In a stable up in town."

"You'd better go an' git 'em an' bring 'em down here, for I reckon you have to pay for their keep up thar."

Two of the boys went after the horses, and the other accompanied his father to secure the fish left on the trot-line.

It was finally agreed upon that the boys should assume the name of Brown and pass as sons of their father. About two hundred dollars was the cash capital of the brothers, which was mostly in the keeping of James. His plan was to move upon some farm, far out in the country, and as soon as practicable, "for," reasoned he, "this place is too public and not at all safe for us."

A few days after they were residing upon a farm ten miles from Catlettsburg, in Virginia.

As the boys had for a year or two been dealing in a manner scarcely as satisfactory or profitable to others as themselves, it was not surprising that they felt some uneasiness and, like their father, were fain to avoid intimate relations with the world beyond the imperative demands of business.

The relation of father and son having been in great measure lost by years of separation, it was not unnatural for James, the eldest of the boys, to assume the position of director in all transactions and movements. When he proposed, the others agreed; when he disagreed, propositions were unceremoniously tossed overboard.

A few weeks after their removal to the country, James grew restless, and for the purpose of extracting money from his father, said that it was not best for them to remain together; that he would go to Kentucky, buy a farm, and if anything should go wrong they could all come there and live. The father, who was beginning to grow restive, approved the suggestion, the more cordially because he believed that James possessed the means to make the proposed purchase. But when the latter remarked that the only difficulty in the way would be raising money for the venture, the mercury of the old man's approbation dropped to zero, and he could not see the necessity for a change at present. He finally grudgingly gave one hundred dollars, and James departed for Kentucky.

CHAPTER XI. A Visit Home—Removal to Kentucky

Pinkney and Gilliam remained on the farm with their father during the spring and summer, and during the fall paid a brief visit to their old home in Tennessee. They imparted no information to any save the immediate family as to where they had been and what doing. There was some alloy in the pleasure of the old lady upon hearing of her husband, for, although the boys were careful as possible in mentioning the fact that their father had a woman keeping house for them, she, true to the instinctive penetration peculiar to the married of her sex, understood it all, and in that other woman recognized the usurper of her place.

The boys told their old friends that they had heard nothing of their father, and that James had left them for parts unknown, and that they had not heard from him since his departure.

Time had not been idle during their absence and had wrought many changes in persons and things.

Many of their playmates had married and gone from the neighborhood. Others had died. Strange stock grazed upon the old familiar pastures, and the farm was in a state of dilapidation. Fences were down, gates off their hinges and propped up with rails, drawbars were displaced, and the old gun had rusted in its rack. Sister Anna was married, and mother and Polly were alone. The son-in-law, Nathan Frizzle, and Moses and Ab Hopper had been assisting them, but the assistance was meager and given with reluctance. Such abandonment, with all its attendant circumstances, was a sting in the core of all the earthly pleasures of the mother and daughter. The fountain of sympathy was unstirred in the breasts of visiting boys. How greatly worse than "fits for treason, stratagem, and spoils," were they.

"O, you've come back, and I'm so glad!" had exclaimed the overjoyed mother. "You mustn't go off and leave us by ourselves no more, will you? No, no! you've come back to stay with us now, me and little Polly. Don't you think she has growed a heap? I know you come back because we're alone and you wanted to see us; and we wanted to see them, didn't we, Polly? But you stayed away so long I was afeard you would never come back. How foolish I was to think that, then I knowed you was my own dear boys and loved your old mother."

Saying which, the fond old creature embraced them both long and heartily, but all to no purpose, for, without concern for her condition, they had left her a few years before to shift for herself. And this was their welcome home! O, the unselfishness of a mother's undying love! Too good, too pure, too holy and divine to sweeten and enlarge the immortal soul of any other human being upon the face of the earth!

"Well," said Pinkney, "I don't know so well about that. We'll stop around here awhile and see how things work, and if all right, perhaps we will stay."

They attended corn-huskings, frolics, etc., for a week or more, and then made preparations for departure. Gulliam told his mother that he and Pink had "big arrangements abroad," and he reckoned they had best be seeing about them.

"My dear ones," she exclaimed, "you won't go off and leave me again, will you? Stay! do stay! I can't live without you near me!"

Polly also interceded with them with all of a loving sister's affectionate pleading, but it all availed nothing. The hearts of the young men were not to be melted by a mother's and sister's tears and prayers.

"Here's Moses and Ab, and pshaw! what's this feller's name that married Anna? They can get you all you want and keep you up. I reckon, and that's enough in such a place as this, the Lord knows. What's the use of our staying around here doing nothing, I should like for you to tell me; When we can make all we want up in old Virginny and Kaintuck?" said Gulliam.

"Just stay here, my dear boys," cried the lonely woman, "with your poor old mother, and you needn't do anything you don't want to, for Sis and me will do all the work. We just don't want you to leave us again."

"Well, Pink, that's a pretty good offer from the old lady, but then there's no fun to be had around here and, for my part, I am going," said Gulliam.

Moses, who had heard of their intention to return, came in about that time, and finding all importunities useless, told them that if they were entirely destitute of feeling—if they had no love in the world for their own mother, and sister—why, the sooner they left, the better, and, for his part, he had nothing further to say. He then told his mother not to insist. Said he, "I'll take care of you and Poll, and Pink and Gullie can do what they please. They can go or stay, and I don't care a durn which they do."

"When we want your advice, we'll ask you for it," said Pinkney angrily.

"Yes," retorted Moses, "and you can get it without asking for it, and not only that, but a good deal more, as for that matter. And I now say to you both, that you have no love for any of us, as you have clearly shown. And further than that, you will never come to any good end, for neither of you is worth the powder and lead it would take to kill you. And this is all I have to say to you."

He turned away from them and walked into the yard.

It was the middle of the afternoon. The boys caught their horses. Polly had accompanied them to the stable, begging them not to be angry with her and mother, for they could not help wanting them to stay. They spoke kindly to her but said that Moses might go to the devil.

Half an hour later, bidding all good-bye and promising to write often, they started on the road to Cattletsburg, bearing many messages of love to their father.

A few days of constant travel brought them to their destination. The old man devoured with greediness the news from home. After special inquiries about each member of the household, he asked if they had heard anything from James. They replied in the negative, and in turn asked him if James had not written to him.

"No," the old man replied, "an' he never will. I've lost all confidence in Jim. He's not the right kind o' boy or he'd a-let us heard from him before now."

Although Mr. Brown was much exercised over the probable loss of his money he had advanced to James, he said nothing about it to any one except his two sons. In regard to his transactions Mrs. Brown knew little beyond what came under her immediate observation. She never meddled with outdoor affairs, for she fully comprehended the kind of material with which she had to deal; her dependence, and the utter futility of any effort she might make to change the drift of the weakest purpose that floated in the minds of these men.

It was hers simply to hear and obey, and this obedience was rendered with such cheerfulness and readiness that Mr. Brown, if not somewhat devoted to her, felt at least the necessity of her presence and companionship as providing the few pleasures in life he enjoyed.

The boys were induced by their father to remain upon the farm with him during the year 1836.

It was nearly twenty months before they received a letter from James. He wrote from Montgomery County, Kentucky, stating that he had been looking around for a suitable place and at length had found one in that county; that he would like for his father, Pink and Gullie to come as soon as they could, "But," he added, "don't bring the woman with you."

"There, now," said Pink, "that settles her hash. I'm like Jim. I think we can do very well without her. She's mighty in the way, and we have to hide from her whenever we want to talk. So, d———."

"Well, she's not in my way," said Mr. Brown, "an ef you boys don't like her you kin take the less of her. She don't concern any of you, nohow."

"What do you say we must do, then?" said Pink. "You know Jim'll cut up like the devil if we take her down there with us, and if we are going we had better be getting ready, for the crop season has almost begun."

It was the settled conviction of the old man and boys that it was to their interest to go, and the disposition of Mrs. Brown was the only difficult question to be previously settled. It would not do to kill her; nor yet would it mend matters to leave her behind; for she was possessed of some facts which she might in resentment be inclined to disclose.

"Ef we kin git a girl to stay with her, perhaps she will be willin' to stop here on my promisin' to come back after her," said Mr. Brown.

The proposition was made to her, and with that reluctance which indicates true affection she finally agreed to the arrangement.

The Kentucky fever was running so high as to breed an unrestrainable impatience to get off. Some of the property was sold off, and it was proposed to sell old Kit, along with the rest, but the father objected. He said she had been a faithful animal and had served him well, and he intended to keep her as long as she lived. Pinkney hired a black girl from one of the nieghbors to stay with his reputed mother for three months. Then promising to return for her at the expiration of that time, they all left for Kentucky, arriving in Montgomery on the tenth day of February, 1837. They brought with them Kit and her colt, the latter a beautiful stallion two years old. He was black as a raven, except a star on his forehead, and Pinkney proudly declared that money could not buy him.

James, at the request of his father, had assumed the name of Hooper, and over this name he had written to the old man. So now the whole of them passed by that name in Montgomery. James had a wife and was keeping house upon a farm he had bought from Mr. George Case, and for which he had contracted to pay twelve hundred dollars, one-half of the purchase money being paid cash in hand. Of his marriage he told but little, only saying that his wife was Miss Drew, of Illinois, in which state he had passed most of his time since leaving Virginia, until he came to Montgomery County.

They were all pleased with James's purchase and concluded to make their future home in that county. Their brother, Ab, who had been "lying around loose" in Tennessee, had been written to by James and requested to come out, and was confidently expected to arrive at any moment, but he did not come until a week after the arrival of his father and brothers. He soon became enamored with a Miss Stull, of the neighborhood; married her, and returned to Tennessee. While in Kentucky he passed as a nephew of the old man, John Hooper, and a cousin to the boys.

The two young men possessed compact and handsome figures, habitually dressed well, and invariably made a favorable impression upon strangers. Among the belles of the county nothing was heard but Mr. Pinkney Hooper this and Mr. Gulliam Hooper that, and to such an extent that they became imbued with the belief that they were the chief indispensables on the occasion of every social gathering. It was very natural, too, that in proportion to their increase in popularity among the ladies was their decrease in estimation among the young men. This is true, as a general rule, among both sexes the world over. But particularly it is prominently observable among the gentler, fairer, and better portion of our race. Let a young lady become the object of admiration and magnet of attraction to the gentlemen of a town or county neighborhood, and she at once becomes the target of hatred from her sisters, and envy, jealousy, and their vile and inseparable companion, slander, dog her every step, and if she be at all sensitive, fill her life with misery unutterable over her good name assailed and her reputation trampled in the mud.

If the Angel of Tears were gathering the holiest drops to sparkle in her diadem of innocence, sweet hope, and bright promise, she would hover long at the couch of the envied woman, for such drops are there in lavish profusion.

CHAPTER XII. Shooting of Willis Roberts

Late one afternoon, about the middle of August, Willis Roberts, a prominent citizen of Montgomery County, while riding along the public road near the residence of the Hoopers, was shot through the shoulder by some one concealed in Hooper's cornfield. The weapon used was a rifle. The ball struck near the lower point of the shoulder blade, passed through the body, and lodged under the skin above the right breast. The wounded man rode a short distance, then lost consciousness and fell from his horse. A neighbor and friend came along and found him prostrate and bleeding in the road where he had fallen.

The wound was severe but not mortal, and it was not long before he was convalescent and able to give the particulars, as far as he knew, of the attempted murder. He unhesitatingly charged James Hooper, with whom he had not been on good terms for some time, with the deed. He positively asserted that he saw the man he accused running through the corn immediately after the gun was fired. Upon this information, Hooper was arrested and brought before the county judge at Mt. Sterling and held by that official to answer an indictment at the next term of the circuit court which was to convene only one month from that date. He found no difficulty in giving the required bond for his appearance, and when the court convened was formally indicted for malicious shooting and wounding with intent to kill. Roberts swore positively upon the trial that the accused was the man who shot him; that he saw him running through the cornfield, gun in hand, immediately after the shot was fired. Pinkney and Gulliam were introduced for the defense, and they testified with equal positiveness that during the whole afternoon of the day of which the shooting occurred James Hooper was with them at the house, fully a half mile distant from the field where the would-be assassin was ambushed, and that they saw a man about the size of their brother pass the house that same afternoon, and to the best of their recollection he carried a gun upon his shoulder. Their testimony created a doubt in the minds of the jury as to Hooper's guilt, and they accordingly rendered a verdict of acquittal.

There was scarcely a man in the community, notwithstanding the result of the trial, who did not believe him guilty of the attempted assassination, and so strong were his neighbors in the belief that they occasionally threw out some unmistakable hints, which were so uncomfortable to Hooper that he and his wife, under cover of night, left soon afterward for Indiana. This was in October, 1839.

The old man had returned to Virginia more than a year before these occurrences. The Hooper boys had become acquainted with the people, but the latter lacked much of being acquainted with them and their antecedents. They were, indeed, cordially hated by most of their neighbors, as they were suspected of dishonesty in their dealing, and were regarded as dangerous in the dark.

Outlaw of Grayson County

During the past two years Pinkney and Gulliam had worked upon the farm and traded in live stock on a small scale. They would sometimes absent themselves to distant and unknown sections of the country and not return for several weeks. It was remarked by some of the neighbors that they left with but little and returned full-handed. How they obtained their money, the most intimate of their acquaintances never knew. During the nine months immediately preceding the flight of James, Pinkney had been living with Thomas Grubb, a substantial and enterprising farmer, who lived some ten miles distant from his brother, Gulliam's home, but their intimate relations in trade and other matters were not suffered to lag.

It was in this spring when Pinkney, with his stallion, came to Grubbs's house. He remained there a few months, during which time he succeeded in imposing upon the credulity of the later, and so ingratiated himself into the good graces of the honest farmer that the latter, being lonesome with only his wife and negroes, asked Pinkney to remain with him all the time; in fact, to make his house his home.

Grubbs was a great stock trader and had grown very wealthy by the business. He was also a Christian gentleman, passionately devoted to his church, and was exceedingly popular with the people of his county. On one occasion he employed Pinkney to assist him in taking a large drove of mules and horses to Pennsylvania, and he had evinced such sound judgment in their management and sale that Grubbs not only regarded him as one of the best business men in Montgomery County but also as the soul of honesty, and hesitated on no occasion, when pertinent, to give free expression to this opinion. Some of Grubbs's friends, however, volunteered some very wholesome advice, apparently so well grounded as to shake his confidence somewhat in the man. But about this time a protracted meeting was being held by Grubbs's church, and Pinkney, having discovered that his greatest weakness lay in his church partiality and religious prejudices, attended the meetings with great regularity and well simulated interest, and one evening responded to the call for mourners. He soon made a bright (?) profession, and was received into the church and reinstated into the full confidence of Grubbs.

Gulliam also had been a frequent attendant upon the services, and on the evening of Pinkney's profession accompanied him home and spent several days at the Grubbs house. The brothers stayed in a room remote from that occupied by their host and hostess. Their light was early extinguished to create the impression that they had retired for the night, but they sat up in the darkness and conversed long and earnesly.

"I think, Gullie," said Pinkney, "that we've got a good thing of this. You've noticed that the old fellow seems to think a good deal of me now, and he'll do anything in the world that I want him to. These rascals about here had talked to him so much against me that I was satisfied he was looking around to find some one else to buy his stock and take charge of his farm. But you see I knew just how to reach him, and if I know anything, have been a little too sharp for the boys."

"It's the sharpest thing out," admiringly responded Gulliam.

"Yes, and we'll make it pay, you mark that," added the other.

"Go on," said Gulliam.

"Well, there is this, you know. He has already spoken for some stock, and if he had liked me as well as at first would have had me buying for him now. I am pretty sure he will say something to me about it in the morning. I judge from what he said to me tonight when I joined the church. I am going to appear rather humble, yet independent, when he speaks to me on the subject. I know exactly how to work him. He hasn't but about five hundred dollars in the house that I know of. I could get that tonight, but I have a better thing a little ahead. When I begin to buy I am going to do it fast and a heap of them. I think he'll put me in charge of a hundred head or more, and if he does, I'll be damned if it isn't all I ask."

"That was a pretty good swear for a Methodist," laughingly said Gulliam. "But," he added, "We had better go to bed, for it is past midnight. Yet I'm not a bit sleepy."

Next morning they were greeted with unusual warmth by Grubbs and his wife. After breakfast the old gentleman told Pinkney that he wanted him to go to work now and get up a drove of stock, and that, too, as soon as he could get ready.

"I have been thinking something about the matter," said Pinkney, "and had concluded, in the event you should speak favorably to me, to decline and try to make some other arrangements. I have received a proposition from another source, in another county, which I had thought of accepting."

"Why, what is that all about?" exclaimed Mr. Grubbs in astonishment.

"You know, Mr. Grubbs," was the reply, "that I have been talked about so much around here that I have lost your confidence, and of course I don't want to work for a man who would think that I am dishonest."

"That's perfectly right," said Mr. Grubbs. "But don't you know, my young friend, that I pay no attention to what people say? I am going to do as I please, regardless of other people's advice. I want you, and if you are willing to stay with me, you can strike out to-day and buy. Come, now; I'm a minuteman; what do you say?"

"I'll work for you, sir," was the response.

"Enough said," and Grubbs entered the house. Pinkney and Gulliam repaired to the stable.

"I told you," said Pinkney, "that I knew how to work him. How do you like it? We must talk fast, for I do not want him to see us engaged in any whispered conversation. So you catch your horse and start off and wait for me about a mile out on the road. Go up the creek, out there, about two or three hundred yards in the woods. I'll be along and see you presently."

An hour later and the brothers were together in the woods.

"Now, Pink, how much is there at the bottom of this? Two thousand, you guess?" queried Gulliam.

"Two thousand!" exclaimed the other, "yes, seven of them at least!"

"That's enough," said Gulliam, "and it's the first sure chance at a big thing we've ever had. Now if we can only work the thing smart. I haven't been saying much, but I've done a good deal of thinking, and I just say it is a damn piece of foolishness for a fellow to be poor when he can just as easily be rich."

"That's my notion, too," said Pinkney, "and this is an opportunity. As soon as I start off with the stock I want you to gather up all the debts that are owing to us around here and strike out for another point. Find some obscure section of the country—a place where you, and pap, and myself can live together in some peace. I don't care where it is, so that it is far enough from here for us never to be found out. When you can find such a place write me at Catlettsburg. Do this at once. It will not take me many weeks to do my part. When I get your letter I expect to be full-handed, and will bring the old man along right away."

With this understanding between them, the brothers separated.

Pinkney employed Ab Robinson and Obediah Curry to assist him in buying, and also in driving the stock to market. Grubbs asked him why he did not employ his brother to help him. He replied that Gulliam was no judge of stock and that he was not in good health anyway. Grubbs affirmed that he had noticed something appeared to be the matter with him but had no idea what it was. Then, after expressing hearty sympathy for the young man, requested Pinkney to invite him to come and stay at his house until he (Pinkney) should return.

Pinkney made a plausible excuse for his brother, knowing that an acceptance of the hospitable invitation would conflict with the plans matured and understood between them and interfere with their future course, already decided upon. Besides, Gulliam already had enough to do in arranging matters necessary and preparatory to discovering an obscure and safe rendezvous for the family after the perpetration of their contemplated robbery of the too-confiding Grubbs. He afterward met Gulliam and informed him of the old farmer's request, at the same time telling him that it would never do to accept, but advised him to ride over there occasionally and keep on the good side of Grubbs. Gulliam readily assented to this suggestion and then, after concerting a few more matters relative to their future meeting, the brothers parted, each going his separate way to perform his part in the projected swindle.

A few weeks later and Pinkney, Robinson and Curry were crossing the Pennsylvania line and approaching the city of Philadelphia, having in charge Grubb's mules. They stopped for a few days within twenty miles of the city to rest the stock, as Pinkney said, and to feel the market. Leaving the others in charge of the drove, Pinkney rode into Philadelphia, spent a night there and returned. He had, however, acquainted himself with the state of the market and met some of the men on whom he held notes, as the agent for Grubbs, for collection. The whole of these claims were upon men of stability and substance, were equivalent to cash and amounted in the aggregate to five thousand and twenty-five dollars. About two thousand of it were upon parties residing in New Jersey.

The time had now arrived for the execution of Pinkney's plans. He selected about fifty head of the largest and most valuable of the stock, and making a separate drove of them, directed Robinson and Curry to take charge of the remainder, drive them to Monroe County, dispose of them to the best advantages they could, and report to him as soon as practicable in Philadelphia, assigning as a reason for his course that in the northern part of the state small and indifferent stock would bring almost as much in the market as the larger and better ones, while in Philadelphia they would scarcely find sale at any price. He then assisted them for five or ten miles on their route. Returning, he hired a couple of hands and started for the city. A few hours after his arrival he made a lump sale of the fifty mules to Rowland Hart (one of the former purchasers of a drove from Grubbs) at the round price of one hundred and twenty-five dollars.

"Now," said Pinkney, "here are some notes, one upon you for nine hundred dollars and the others all on good men, I presume, and as I am in a hurry to get with the other boys who have gone north with a drove of eighty mules, Ill let you have them at a reasonable discount."

"What do you call a reasonable discount?" asked Mr. Hart.

"Well," was the reply, "what do you say yourself?"

"No," said Hart, "I won't fix the price on another man's property."

"Then I will," said Pinkney. "You may have the whole for five thousand."

Hart was a man of remarkable penetration, but he failed to discover any indication of uneasiness in Pinkney's manner. He hesitated and calculated some time before answering. Finally he declined the proposition, paid for the stock he had purchased, took in his own note, and Pinkney, with a pleasant grasp of the hand and a gracious smile, bade him "good evening."

CHAPTER XIII. Dock Brown Appears

Gulliam remained but a short time in Montgomery after Pinkney left. Having hastily wound up his business, he was a week afterward the center of attraction on a big muster-day at the residence of Benjamin Deweese in Grayson County, eleven miles west of Leitchfield on the Hartford road.

The sensation a young, handsome and well-dressed stranger would create on this and all similar occasions, at that day, and in that society, was even greater than that we notice now at our country picnics and barbecues. Most persons have seen the "Who-is-that-fellow?" at a barbecue, and have noticed, too, the pleasure he could not conceal at feeling that he is the observed of all observers, and the air of graceful nonchalance he assumes as the half-whispered compliments of the fair ones reach his ear. Such was Gulliam on this day, as he proudly stood by his superb young black horse, the colt of old Kit.

With pleasure we now introduce Gulliam Hooper to the readers as the veritable Doctor G. Brown, or Dock Brown (as he was afterward universally designated), the hero of this story—the younger brother at the board tree, whose heart quivered with grief when his father disappeared in the dark Tennessee forest.

That "the sins of the parents are visited upon their children" is susceptible of several constructions—three at least. First, hereditary physical disease; second, hereditary evil inclinations; the evil of influence or bad example. One or both of the first are accepted generally by the religious world as orthodox; that is, as being true rendering of that declaration of Holy Writ. Science has demonstrated the truth of the first. The second is purely metaphysical, and is accepted as only belief, resting upon the broad foundation of faith. The third comes under the immediate observation, but whether it is embraced in the declaration quoted is a moot question. It is not unreasonable to believe that all are included.

It is not infrequently asserted that there is nothing said or done in this life but has an eternal influence for good or evil. If so, what must have been the effect of the father's crime in the woods upon the young and tender natures of his boys? The delicate flower, pinched and shiveled by the cold, frosty breath that called it forth, can "never bloom more." The shirt-sleeves of the younger boy were never again moistened by tears of genuine sorrow. They were then and there staunched, and forever. Nine-tenths of the world's misery has been occasioned by the unguarded words and hasty actions. How much better it would be for mankind were we all to stop and think before speaking words we can never recall, and stay the hand raised in anger before it smites. Could this be done the world over, what a glorious revolution would be produced in the great heart of humanity.

Dock Brown was a man whose villainy, perfidy, turpitude, and blackness of heart, and whose heinous secret and open crimes have had but few parallels in the history of our race. But the unpretending, unassuming people in the Deweese and Pine Knob neighborhood judged a man solely from his appearance and manners. If he looked and behaved well, he was received into full fellowship, and no questions asked about his antecedents. In a word, every stranger was regarded by them as honest, at least until the contrary appeared. Such has always been a noble characteristic of Kentuckians, until the close of the late war, which was a revolution not only in state and national politics but also in our social domestic affairs. But there is nothing strange in this.

CHAPTER XIV. Uncle and Nephew

There was a family resemblance among the Hoppers, alias Hoopers, Browns, etc., and through the remotest degrees of consanguinity. Those who remember them also remember the uniformity of expression in their eyes. Moses Edwards very closely resembled Dock Brown's father, and Dock Brown himself would very easily have passed anywhere as the brother of Moses. There was a mutual recognition of this likeness between them at the breakfast table, but neither spoke a word upon the subject. It was a silence of unpleasant suspense to Dock. He had mapped out a plan of future action, which would largely depend upon the impression he would create upon the Edwards family. Upon Edwards this likeness had a remarkable effect, though he gave no outward sign of the tumult that suddenly raged within him. It brought up the long buried and half-forgotten past, with its dark secrets and events that came to haunt him in spite of himself, and all called up by the sight of the face of the young stranger who sat at his board. And yet he spoke not a word that would betray his mental unrest.

After concluding their meal, Moses Edwards and his guest took their hats and walked out to the stable and beyond, with as full an understanding of each other's purposes as though they had settled upon it after full and free discussion. This is no psychological phenomenon but a natural and perceptible affinity existing between similar natures brought into close proximity, and is observable through the entire race of man to the close and intelligent student of human nature. It is also as full and perfect in the spiritual and mental worlds, and rules and controls all the passions belonging to them "as with a rod of iron." Love, anger, hatred, fear, revenge, greed, etc., are its abject subjects.

Reaching a point where they could converse without fear of interruption or being overheard, Edwards broke the silence that had been maintained since leaving the house by asking the young man if he was really from Pennsylvania. Dock replied evasively that he was from many places but had no place in particular.

"But say, don't be afraid to speak out," said Edwards earnestly, "for I have something to tell in case my suspicions are correct. I want to know what your father's name is."

"I'd rather hear from you first," said the other.

"I heard you say that your name was Gulliam, and I want to know if you ever knew Gulliam Hopper."

"Well, y-e-s!" exclaimed the now astonished young man, "I used to know a man by that name in Tennessee."

"Did he live at McMinnville?" queried Edwards, scarcely able to restrain his excitement.

"Near there," was the answer.

"Is he alive now?" was the next question.

"He was the last time I heard from him, which was a month ago."

"Ain't you a-kin to him?"

"Hold on, now," said Dock, whose coolness had returned, and who was now both wary and watchful. "You are going too fast to suit me. If you want to find out anything more about me you will have to first explain yourself."

"All this is private, of course," said Edwards, recognizing the justness of Dock's objection to further catechising without an explanation of his object. "I am Gulliam Hopper's brother."

"I am his son," said Dock.

CHAPTER XV.   Pinkney's Success.   Change of Name and Arrival

Pinkney cashed Grubb's checks and notes in banks, the latter at a reasonable discount, and went to New Jersey. Here he made close collections of notes negotiable and payable at a Trenton bank, which wound up Grubb's unfinished business in the eastern market, and then, with seven thousand dollars of ill-gotten money, hurried back to Catlettsburg. Shortly after his arrival there he received a letter from Dock, bearing the Leitchfield postmark. The contents were satisfactory in every particular and sufficient to endorse hasty preparations upon the part of the old man, his reputed wife, and Pinkney to start to Pine Knob. The letter suggested the impropriety of all going together, and thought it best that he should go first. He wrote to Dock, giving him a hint of his success, and requested him to meet him at Cloverport on a certain named day. This letter was superscribed: Dr. G. Brown, Leitchfield, Grayson Co., Kentucky."

A week or ten days after mailing his letter, Pinkney boarded a steamer at Cincinnati. A short time before the signal to pull out was struck on the bell, he was standing on the cabin deck, leaning against the guards, watching the roustabouts loading freight below, when he was approached and addressed by an old acquaintance from Mt. Sterling. The latter came up from behind and called his name before Pinkney observed his presence.

Pinkney swiftly turned at the mention of his name, trembling for a moment, with his right hand clutching a dagger in his bosom, but immediately recovered his self-control as he recognized the speaker, apologized for his momentary excitement, passed the usual compliments of the day, and asked Mr. Simms (for that was the name of the gentleman) how Grubbs and other acquaintances in Montgomery were getting along. Simms told him that Grubbs was very uneasy about him; that he had heard nothing from him since Robinson and Curry returned, and that they had told some very hard stories about him—that he had run off with most of the stock, had collected Grubb's money, and was in parts unknown.

Pinkney, with smiling indifference, said, "Well, they are nice fellows to tell such a damned lie as that when I told them all about my arrangements, which were to sell the stock, collect all the money I could, and return home by the way of Louisville. I am going home tomorrow, or, rather, I shall start tomorrow, and will get home in a few days. When are you going?"

"I shall not go for several weeks, as I am on my way to New York. It may be a month before I return."

"Ah, well, then I'll beat you home. I was going to ask you to tell Grubbs that you saw me and that all was right, but I'll see him first. This is bad treatment, but I'll make it all right and settle with Curry and Robinson for their lies."

Simms agreed that it was a shameful outrage and that he would not blame Pinkney for anything he might do in vindication of his good name. Then expressing a wish that all would turn out all right, he bade him good-bye, stepped off the boat and went up town.

The boat reached Louisville and, fortunately for Pinkney, made close connection with a southbound steamer which was tying at the New Albany wharf, which enabled him to reach Cloverport near the appointed time. Dock met him on deck when the boat landed. He had brought two horses, one for himself and the other for Pinkney.

They left Cloverport that afternoon and came out about fifteen miles on the Bowling Green road to James Howard's This place was well known and a favorite stopping place for all wagoners between Bowling Green and Cloverport, which was then the terminus of the great thoroughfare of trade and travel for all the upper Green River country, to whom its genial proprietor was familiarly known as "Uncle Jimmy Howard." It was a perfect model of the ideal good old fashioned country home, where freely flowed the buttermilk and honey. If a man stopped with Uncle Jimmy once, he was certain to stop again and again. Many who read this will cordially endorse the above and, with the author, regret that space and impertinence to the thread of the story forbid a just tribute to the sterling worth of the kindly old host of that famous old country caravansary—"Half-Way House," beyond the Falls of Rough.

Pinkney was now no longer Hopper or Hooper, but P. H. Brown. The change in his name was made immediately upon the reception of Dock's letter and was well understood and readily adopted when he reached Cloverport.

They reached the home of Moses Edwards the next day at noon, but finding no one at home, went over to Pine Knob meeting house to hear preaching by Rev. Charles Stuteville. Those who could not get seats in the house occupied logs and outdoor benches, while others were passing to and from the spring with gourds and pails of water for the thirsty sisters.

Such was the picture that presented itself to the Browns as they rode up and dismounted. Every eye outdoors and many inside were turned upon them. They did not look like other people—did not act like other people. They were termed "some o' yer town folks." "Who's that feller with Dock Brown?" was the question in the minds of all, and which was expressed by many. They hitched their horses and came up to a log on which several men were sitting, among whom was Isaac Deweese Sr., and D. S. Carroll, who are yet living in that part of the county.

Pinkney was introduced to all of them, and was so polite, graceful and pleasant in smiles and words that he soon won their admiration despite his costly and envied apparel.

Preaching was finally over — for even the lungs of the pioneer preacher required a season of rest, whatever befell the ears of his congregation during a two or three hour discourse—and the women speedily and deftly prepared a besket dinner to which the Browns, by cordial invitation from many, did ample justice. Through the gallantry of Carroll and Bennett Pirtle they made the acquaintance of the best young women on the ground and took active part with them in the afternoon singing school.

CHAPTER XVI. John Brown Arrives

According to arrangements made by Pinkney, Dock left next day to meet his father and the old lady at West Point in Hardin County. The day designated for the meeting was the twelfth of September, but that day passed and nothing was seen or heard of the old people. Dock, growing impatient, rode on toward Louisville with the hope of meeting them on the way.

Late in theafternoon as he was nearing the suburbs of the city, a small one-horse go-cart appeared in sight, with a man driving, seated in front. It was John Hopper. The old lady was sitting upon a bundle of old quilts in the bottom of the vehicle. Dock's inquiries about the cause of detention was answered by the old man.

"Ole Kit died yestiddy," said he, "an' I had to swap the waggin for this concern, so that one hoss could pull us. An' it was a long time afore I could make the raise. Poor Kit! she's gone at last!"

"Yes," said Dock, "but you couldn't expect her to live always. You see, she was—let me see—she was nearly twenty years old."

"Nigh on to twenty-one," said the old man sadly.

"Where did you leave her?"

"A lettle this side o' B'argrass. The old gal, here, has bin cryin' 'bout her ever since."

"Pshaw!" exclaimed Dock, "there's no use in that. Let the poor old creature go. I've got something else on my mind now that is more important and weighs heavier than old Kit. I forgot to ask Pink about it. Did you ever get any of that money back you let Jim have?"

"Nary a cent of it. He an' Case rode back, unbeknowns to me, an' Case paid him back what he'd paid on the lan' an' thet was the last of it. Jim didn't act fair with me. I thought I tole you. I know I tole Pink all about it," was the reply.

"I want it understood," said Dock. "that I have no further use for him, even if he is my brother. If I'd known he was such a rascal as that, Pink and me never would have kept him out of the penitentiary in that Roberts case. If it hadn't been for us he'd gone there certain, and he knows it. I haven't heard from him since he left, and I don't want to hear from him any more."

"Don't you know whar he is?" asked his father.

"No," was the response. "But there is something else I want to tell you. I never wrote to you nor Pink about it, and never told him until we met at Cloverport the other day. It's this: You know I've heard you and mother speak of your brother Moses?"

"Yes. Well?"

"Well, do you know where he is?"

"No, I don't. Do you?"

"Yes."

"Where is he?"

"He lives down there in Grayson County where we are going, near Pine Knob. He goes by the name of Moses Edwards."

"How did you fin' him out?"

"I'd let you guess, but then you'd never guess it in the world."

"Yes, I kin. I'll bet you've called yerself Hopper, or sed somethin' 'bout the name sometime, an' he's hearn of it."

"No, no; I never have. You can't guess, I see that. That wasn't the way at all."

"How, then?"

"Well, in the first place I saw two of his boys one day, and they looked so much like our family that I got acquainted with them. Next morning their father (Uncle Moses) and me took a walk, and he told me who he was. You look just alike, and he says I look like you used to, and he thought of you as soon as he laid eyes on me."

"Well, well. Does he know we're comin'?"

Outlaw of Grayson County

"Yes, and says he will be the gladdest in the world to see you. But then, he says, it won't do for you to pass as brothers. We've fixed it up for you to be an old acquaintance, and nothing more."

"Did he norate to you what made him change his name?"

"No, but he said maybe he'd tell me some day, but not now, and I said nothing more to him on the subject."

"Thet was right," said the old man. "I know all about it but there's no needcessity for you and Pink to know. Did you tell him why our names was changed?"

"No, and don't intend to."

"I'm glad o' thet. I want to manage thet myself."

"What name do you go by now?" asked Dock.

"John Brown. I've been goin' by thet name ever since I went back to ole Virginny," was the answer.

"There's no use of changing any more now," said the son. "You are to be our father, and the old lady here, our mother."

"Thet's all right," said the old man. "What kind o' place is Pine Knob?"

"It's a backwoods sort of place and is called Pine Knob because of the tall cliffs and knobs covered with pines. It's a mighty hilly country, and has more caves and dens than any place I ever saw. It'll just suit us all around."

At the close of this conversation they were within a few miles of Salt River, near a farm which is still in cultivation and borders upon the line of the Louisville, Paducah and Southwestern Railway. Here, weary and greatly fatigued, they encamped for the night.

They resumed their journey at daylight next morning, but took the wrong road, and did not discover their error until they had nearly reached Elizabethtown, and thus it happened that it was midnight—and intensely dark—when they reached the eastern hill-top of Big Clifty, ten miles from Leitchfield. They had traveled far, and would have gladly rested during the remainder of the night, but Dock's impatience could not be restrained.

Big Clifty is the name of a small creek, and its name is quite suggestive of the character of the stream it is. Save subterranean passages, it is doubtless the darkest watercourse in the state. Snakes, frogs, fishes and turtles live and die in its waters, of old age, and never get a glimpse of the sun. Far, far below the average depths, with much unseen, it creeps along with an echoing murmur in its narrow bed, bending and twisting its shallow ripples with the shaggy sides of its rocky shelter—a miniature Lethe— and then on and away among the dismal cliffs of a dark beyond.

Where the tall railway trestle now spans its somber depths was the old road crossing at the time of which we write—and even to this day, for that matter—and at this spot the Browns halted for a brief rest. Dock went below to explore the route, but returned in a few moments greatly frightened, exclaiming:

"This must be hell sure enough! I got down to the branch and crossed over, and as soon as I got on the other side I thought I heard a voice say, 'Gullie, is that you?' I didn't answer but got back up here."

"Didn't you see nothin'?" asked the father.

"See! I'say see. I saw lightning bugs, and that's all a feller can see down there, but———"

There was the sound of a horse's feet on the rocks below them. They came nearer and nearer, until the outline of a man and a horse became visible. There was a sudden halt. Dock, presenting his pistol, demanded, "Who is there?"

"Is that you, Gullie? Are you all here? Pshaw! don't you know?"

"Well, if it ain't Pink," cried Dock. "What do you mean by scaring a body that way?"

"Was that you at the creek a while ago?"

"Yes, it was."

"Well, I didn't know who it was but spoke, thinking maybe it was you, and when you ran up the hill, I felt sorter ticklish myself, though I didn't mean to scare you."

"How did you happen to meet us here?"

Pinkney, who had dismounted, told them of his uneasiness. He had been to Salt River, and there learned that they had taken the Elizabethtown road, and he came back expecting to intercept them at Leitchfield, but failing in that he had started to meet them, and was glad that he had at last done so, even if he had scared them half to death.

They passed through Leitchfield while the town was asleep. About eight o'clock the next morning they arrived at the house of Silas Mahurin, three-quarters of a mile up the valley from the Pine Knob meeting house. Brown and his wife remained there while Pinkney and Dock rode on to inform Moses Edwards of their arrival. A few hours afterward Moses and Martin Edwards came to Mahurin's. They found Brown and his wife asleep, the former on a pallet

Outlaw of Grayson County

under a shade tree in the yard. They were not intentionally disturbed.

The four, the two Edwardses and Pink and Dock seated themselves on the grass in the yard, only a few steps from the pallet on which the old man was resting and sleeping. Moses looked intently at the sleeper, said that Gulliam had changed so much that he———.

"Hush-sh!" exclaimed Pinkney, interrupting him. "You mustn't call his name. Remember that he is John H. Brown and that he is not your brother."

"It's among ourselves," said Moses.

"Yes, but you don't know what it might lead to. We've all got too much at stake to be careless respecting the concealment of our identity."

"Why did he put the 'H' in his name?" asked Edwards.

"We never asked him," replied Pinkney, "but suppose for the same reason that it is in mine."

"For Hopper?"

"For Hopper," was the reply.

When a man is asleep, the general faculties of his mind are sluggish, inactive, and almost totally dormant, and he is oblivious to his surroundings; but the spiritual essence never rests but hovers around and near everything that in any way pertains to its joy or sorrow. So one is in either extreme more easily awakened than when in the intermediate state.

The name "Hopper" fell upon the sleeper's ear, and he instantly awoke and sprang to his feet. He had not fully comprehended the situation before Moses grasped him warmly by the hand. Neither spoke for several seconds, but looked long into each other's face. The recollection of many youthful and manhood pleasures, as well as sad events that led to their separation, crowded the minds of each. At last Brown said: "And this is Moses Edwards?"

"It is," was the reply. "And this is John H. Brown?"

"This is, sir, your old friend, John H. Brown, though changed a heap since you saw him. An', Mose, you, too, have changed more'n consider'ble."

"Yes, I've been through the flint mill. Here's my son, Martin. You never saw him."

"No, I never saw any of your children. How many hev you got?"

"A house full, but none of 'em's any account. Mart, here, is a fair average."

Mrs. Brown and Mrs. Mahurin now made their appearance from the house and were introduced all 'round. The entire party seated themselves and engaged in an animated conversation, which was interrupted by the sight of some one coming toward them across the field.

"It's Silas," said Mrs. Mahurin, but what's he got? Ain't it a deer?"

Silas entered the yard almost before the question was out of her mouth, dragging a large deer he had killed on his way from Caneyville. He soon became acquainted with the new-comers—having been absent when they arrived at his house the previous evening—and divided his game with the Edwardses, who presently left for their home, accompanied by the Browns.

The Browns made their home with Edwards for several weeks, during which time Dock and Pinkney devoted a great deal of time to the young ladies of the neighborhood. They also came to Leitchfield and made the acquaintance of the wealthiest and most influential of the townspeople. They had plenty of money for those days, and were, when they chose to be, young men of extensive and even elegant leisure.

Then Grayson had but few homely daughters. They were, our old men say, "nearly all beauties." Compared with those of the present day, they were inferior in point of education, but they were far superior in physical development, stability and amiability. If they had faults, the greatest was credulity. Alas! for the education of the present day—the polish of the mind and the torture of the body! Alas, for fashion, physical deformity, degeneracy, and premature decay.

CHAPTER XVII. Brief, But Important

Uncle Jimmy Ross, an English gentleman of high puritanic notions, kept the hotel at Leitchfield. Jack Thomas was the circuit and county clerk, and Edwin Thomas, his son, now circuit clerk, was his deputy. William L. Conklin and Jack Thomas were the only lawyers and were alternately appointed county attorney. Dr. A. C. BcBeath and Dr. R. L. Heston were the principal physicians.

Pinkney and Dock Brown traded in horses and cattle. They bought the Mahurin place in the spring of 1842 and built a hewed log cabin for their residence in the valley near the church and spring. The building contained two rooms—one the main or large room, and the other very small, about six by twelve feet. It was built upon the hillside. The smaller room was at the south or lower end, elevated to a level upon a rock wall or foundation. There was also a trap-door near the center of this room, which a close observer would not have detected, and which was unknown even to their most intimate neighbors until after the Browns disappeared. It seemed to be a part of the floor, with its regular joints, and opened into a cellar as dark as a dungeon.

Into this house the four Browns moved and lived in a manner to be detailed hereafter.

CHAPTER XVIII. A Narrow Escape

Thomas Grubbs was a man of firm resolution and iron endurance when stimulated to action by interested motives. He had been outrageously swindled and robbed by a confidential friend and brother in the church, and he spared no means at his command in searching for the villain whom he had suspected too late.

Immediately after Curry and Robinson had returned home from their trip to the east with Pinkney, Grubbs employed some of the best and keenest detectives in the country to visit the principal cities east and north, while he went on to Philadelphia in person to ascertain the amount collected and discover, if possible, some clue that would put him upon the track of the embezzler. All he could learn was the amount of his losses. Returning home, he repaired to Cincinnati, arriving there only a few hours after the boat with Pinkney on board had departed for Louisville, and unfortunately failing to meet Simms, who, it will be remembered, had met Pinkney on the boat and was still in the city.

The hotel registers were carefully scrutinized but yielded no information. The wily rogue had been careful not to register. Grubbs, baffled and discouraged, returned home to await reports from his emissaries, the detectives, and trust to luck for information of a definite character to shape his further efforts. They all came in, one by one, and all they had to report, when summed up, amounted to—nothing.

Letters were then written and dispatched to all parts of the country, giving an accurate description of Pinkney's personal appearance and asking for information as to his whereabouts, but the answers were universally devoid of the desired information.

Several weeks afterward Simms returned to Mt. Sterling and was greatly surprised to learn that Pinkney had not put in his appearance. He told Grubbs and others of his meeting the fugitive on a steamboat at Cincinnati, and how much pained Pinkney appeared to be over the current suspicions concerning his transactions for Grubbs—how he cursed and threatened—and his statement that he was then on his way back by way of Louisville. All of which disclosed the fact that Grubbs and Simms were in Cincinnati at the same time, and almost in the presence of the absconding man. Grubbs stoutly declared that he felt while in the city that he was near Pinkney; that he kept a close eye on everybody; watched the corners and alleys as he passed them, "For," said he, "I would not have been surprised to meet him at any moment, and being sure that he was trying to leave the country with my money, I was afraid that he would try to kill me if he could get the advantage."

Who can understand the wondrous workings of the human mind —the magnetic influence of mind over mind, even in an unconscious proximity? Call it intuition if you please, but there is an unaccountable and mysterious telegraphy going on between soul and soul upon this earth, and sometimes the unseen wires of space are so charged with the magnetic spiritual current as to shock both batteries to consciousness, and that, too, without the mediums of any of the five senses. Then, as the soul is immortal, as is believed by most intelligences, who can say that a dissolution from the body has stopped the electric current? We sometimes speak or think of a person whom we suppose is far from us, but we turn, and lo, he stands in our presence. Now, do not understand me to say that the presence of the individual is the cause of the thought or speech concerning him, for it may be that such an occurrence is but an accidental coincidence.

Simms distinctly remembered the name of the boat on which the meeting with Pinkney occurred but was unable to state whether it was the intention of the latter to travel on it.

Outlaw of Grayson County

Grubbs immediately repaired to Cincinnati and saw and questioned the officers of the boat, but they could give him no information concerning any person that answered the description of Pinkney. The name "Mr. Brown" was upon the clark's register. It was given by Pinkney, was in the clerk's handwriting, and of course, furnished no clue, there being many Mr. Browns traveling about the world. So all inquiries and search were unavailing. And thus years passed.

CHAPTER XIX. Mark Shain

Soon after the Browns settled in their Pine Knob home, men and women, young and old, from various parts of the county, paid them frequent visits during a year or more and until it became clearly evident upon the part of Mrs. Brown that welcome had worn threadbare. She was fond of visitors but never made or returned calls. This unsocial conduct proceeded partly from a sense of her own unworthiness and shame arising from the state of adultery in which she lived, and also in consequence of strict obedience to a positive injunction which emanated from three lords at whose shrines she worshiped, to whose rule she was a willing slave, and whose will was her only law. But the neighbors, ignorant of the domestic relations of the newcomers, looked upon her seclusion and forced exclusiveness as pride, and rated and called the poor creature an aristocrat. Thus it came to pass that the female visitors dropped her from the list and left her alone. The men, however, continued their visits and grew intimate with Pinkney and Dock, and felt greatly complimented when they would participate with them in deer hunting and fox chasing, then the source of pleasure and recreation to the hunters of Grayson.

Among these jovial, free-hearted hunters, and by far the favorite with the Browns, was Mark Shain, who still lives near the Knob. He is seventy-six years of age and keeps his dogs and guns as of old. Having lately regained his long dimmed eyesight, he can use his rifle as well as the best marksman in his neighborhood, and occasionally knocks over a deer or turkey. His neighbors say that he has not been without venison for thirty-five years. He owns eight or ten guns, among which are a few old flint-lock muskets, upon the stocks of which are notches indicating the number of deer, turkeys, wolves and eagles he has killed with them. I have known Shain since my earliest childhood, and ever since I first heard of Daniel Boone have blended their names and lives together. Hon.

DOCK BROWN

Thomas L. Jones, of Newport, Ky., who owns large bodies of land in Shain's neighborhood, visited part of the county last year (1874) and spent several days at Shain's house. He says that in the same length of time he never enjoyed a visit more. And so favorably was he impressed with the appearance and primitive habits of his host that he induced him to have his picture taken in his hunting garb and surrounded by his dogs. This picture, in a costly frame, now adorns the mantel front of Mrs. Jones's parlor. Shain's wife, the loving companion of his young manhood, in the midst of a large family of children and grandchildren, slowly and peacefully passes down the path of healthy old age in blissful contentment.

The hollows and caves of Pine Knob were soon explored by Dock and Pinkney, who became as familiar with their locality and extent as they were with their dwelling house and yard. Big Mouth is the largest cave, and being at the side end of a long ridge, two miles from the Knob, was known to and explored by few save the Browns. This cave has the appearance of being hidden away, as there is nothing near to indicate its half open jaws—15 feet perpendicular and fifty feet wide. Six feet within it is sixty by sixty, extending back eighty feet, thus giving near two hundred and eighty thousand cubic feet of mouth, and at the end of this is the irregular, winding throat which terminates many hundred feet both from the mouth and the surface above.

CHAPTER XX. The Murder of Frank Pugh

One Friday afternoon a stranger came to Leitchfield on horseback. He rode up to a crowd of men seated under the young shade trees in front of the clerk's office and inquired the way to Pine Knob. It so happened that none of the gentlemen present could give him the information, but one of them referred the stranger to Evan Rogers, the postmaster across the square, for direction. The man politely thank them, went to the post office, obtained the desired information, and rode off on the Hartford road.

He was a dark skinned, thin visaged man, about six feet in height, about thirty-five years old, and upon the whole had the appearance of being a well bred gentleman. The animal he bestrode was a large, fine, fat chestnut sorrel mare, of such splendid form and action that she attracted the admiring attention of all who saw her. The clerks' office party called on Rogers to learn something about the stranger. He told them that the man gave the name of Frank Pugh, and claimed to be a half brother to the Brown boys, and said he was going to pay them a visit.

It was after dark when Pugh arrived at the Brown place. His hail at the gate was answered by Dock.

"Does Mr. John Brown live here?" he asked in response to Dock's "What's wanted?"

"Who are you?" queried the latter.

"I'm a stranger, sir," was the reply, "and I want to stay all night with you."

"Light and come in."

The man hitched his horse at the gate and went to the house. The Browns did not know him, but he introduced himself, and after a lengthy conversation, walked out with Dock, whom he told that he was a stranger in this country, was traveling, had a large sum of money with him, and that a man beyond Leitchfield with whom he spent the previous night had referred him to this place for safe quarters, and concluded by saying that he had claimed kin with the family when making inquiries about the road at Leitchfield.

"That's all right," said Dock. "You are perfectly safe here, and we are glad to see you. Walk in and make yourself at home."

As they turned and retraced their steps toward the door, Dock remarked that it was unnecessary to tell any of the family about his money; that it was none of their business. The man agreed with him and they re-entered the house.

After a further brief conversation, Dock arose, and giving Pinkney a wink, excused himself to the stranger and went out, saying that he would go out and attend to Mr. Pugh's horse. Pinkney immediately followed him.

When safely out of earshot of the house, Dock said, "He's an utter stranger here. He lives in Tennessee and is going back shortly. It may be that he's a kind of spy and will tell the Tennessee people all about where we are, so I think we had better settle his hash for him. He's got money, and you can see for yourself what a fine mare this is. What do you say for fixing him?"

"How do you know he's got money?" asked Pinkney.

"Why the fool told me so himself. He said he had about a thousand dollars."

"O, there'll be no difficulty in the world on that score. You go to the house and get your gun, pistol and knife—I've mine with me—ask him to come out and see his horse fed. The old folks will go to bed and to sleep. We will propose a fox chase, and I think from the cut of his eye that he's fond of fun and will go with us. If not, he'll at least be out here at the stable."

"Well," said Pinkney, doubtingly, "s'posing he goes, how'll we manage to keep the old man from finding it out? That's what I'm looking at."

"We'll do it this way. Take him to Big Mouth———"

"But where are the dogs?" interrupted Pinkney. "You know it won't do to start without hounds."

"Here's the trick in a nutshell," said Dock. "We'll tell him that we are going to Mark Shain's after the dogs and tell the old man in the morning that the man got tired in the chase and stopped at Mark's."

"Well, go on now," said Pinkney. "How are we to manage at the cave?"

"Now, that's something we must fix up beforehand," said Dock. "Let me see. It won't do to shoot. We'll have to risk the knife."

"But what'll we do with him after we kill him?"

"Pshaw! Don't ask so many foolish questions. That amounts to nothing now. I'll make the first cut with my knife from behind, just as we enter the cave, and then you'll strike as he turns, and we'll finish the job. The whole thing is understood now. Go on to the house and do as I say."

Pugh had but little to say to the old folks while the boys were

Outlaw of Grayson County

away. When Pinkney returned and opened the door to enter, he sprang instantly to his feet, with pallid face and trembling limbs, the very impersonation of fright. He recovered himself in a moment, as soon as he saw who it was coming in. Pinkney said that he and Dock had concluded to have a fox hunt and added, "You, Mr. Pugh, can go to bed in that room when you wish," pointing to the small room already described, "and we'll be back sometime before midnight. Or, if you choose, we would like to have you with us."

"Why, certainly, I'll go with you," said Pugh, "and thank you, too, for I am exceedingly fond of the chase."

Pinkney went into the little room, got his knife and pistols, concealed them on his person, came out, and the two went to the stable where Dock was waiting for them."

"Mr. Pugh is going with us," Pinkney said to the latter. "You hold the horses while I catch his."

While he was engaged in catching the mare, Mr. Pugh said to Dock: "Hadn't we better tell your brother about the money and leave it at the house?"

"There'll be no harm in it, I guess," was the response. "Yes, I'll tell him."

When Pinkney came out with the mare, Dock said, "Pink, Mr.——, this gentleman—I can't think of your name, sir."

"Pugh."

"Pugh, yes; Mr. Pugh has got some money and thinks it best for us to take care of it for him. Or, rather, wants us to take it to the house and leave it, as it might get lost in the woods. I think myself that it's best; what do you say?"

"Why, leave it, of course," was the reply.

Pugh handed Dock one hundred and fifty dollars in gold and his pocketbook containing nine hundred dollars in bank bills. Dock took them to the house but was careful to keep all in his pocket. He returned, and the three started for the fictitious fox chase. There was no road leading to the Big Mouth, and they went a few hundred yards down the valley in the direction of Shain's, when Dock proposed to cut across a nearer way through the woods. Pinkney, in order to avert all probable suspicion from Pugh's mind, objected, but Dock insisting, all finally concurred and turned off the road. In a very short time thy reached the vicinity of the cave. They rode down a slight declivity and stopped at the mouth.

"Here," said Dock, "is the eighth wonder of the world. Let's go in. We've got plenty of time, and I want to show this cave to Pugh."

"All right," said Pugh.

They alighted, hitched their horses to some neighboring bushes, and approached the entrance. It was bright moonlight without and the blackness of darkness within. They paused as they heard a rapid snapping, and a large gray owl emerged from his lonely roost upon a rocky shelf. His broad wings fanned the brow of the doomed man as the owl flew out of his drear abode.

Pinkney took the lead, saying, "We'll go in a-piece, and I'll strike a light."

He pretended to be feeling for a match but was fastening upon his dagger. Dock grasped his knife, but in drawing it from the sheath the hilt caught in a button hole of his waistcoat, and while he was tearing it loose, Pugh turned around to learn the cause of the ripping noise. He was met by Dock's knife, which, aimed at his throat, struck him on the chin with such force as to snap the blade like glass. The man, stunned by the blow and perhaps paralyzed with terror, staggered and fell at Pinkney's feet, crying in a heart-rending tone:

"Help! O help! My wife—my child—O God! Forgive———"

Pinkney's dagger, by two well directed blows, penetrated first his throat and then his heart, and the victim, struggling in the sand, ceased to speak and soon ceased to breathe. The bloody deed was now done beyond recall. The murderers were alone in the almost palpable darkness with the still body of the dead. They stood like statues for several minutes, neither daring to break the dreadful silence by movement or speech. The owl, from his perch on the dead limb of a tall chestnut hard by, uttered a sepulchral, "Whoo, whoo, whoo-o-oo!" which echoed and reverbrated from every nook and cranny of the cave—now a dismal den of murder.

"This is awful!" finally exclaimed Pinkney.

"No, it isn't," said Dock. "What's the use to talk that way? Nobody knows it. Let's get out of here and walk around a while."

Once out in the moonlight they discovered that their hands and clothing were plentifully bedewed with the fast drying blood of the murdered man. They washed the former in the small branch at the foot of the hill, returned, led the sorrel mare far back in the cave and secured her there; searched the body of the victim, and hid it in a crevice of the cavern. This accomplished, they mounted their horses and hurriedly rode homeward.

Outlaw of Grayson County

Remorse, the legitimate offspring of violated conscience, with its red dagger of remembrance, made its fell and final stroke, severing these two red handed men from all humanity; and thus stripped, the brothers stood in the father's yard fiends incarnate. Their horses were stabled. The waning moon, fast sinking behind the knobs, sent her broken light through the tall pines and upon the blood bespattered garments they wore. The clock on the mantel inside had chimed one, two, three, unheard. Not even an echo from the cave fell upon their ears. There were only whispered plans to avoid the morning's discovery. At length, concluding that if their father should see the blood, they would find it difficult to explain its presence on their clothing, it was agreed that they should enter the house and seek their room as quietly as possible, conceal their bloody apparel, and have it privately washed by the old woman, upon whom they would force the most rigid secrecy.

They lifted the latch. "Who's there?" asked their father.

"Nobody but us," they replied, and passed on into the little room.

"Here," said Dock to the old lady, as she passed their door next morning, "come in here a moment. Where's father?"

"Gone to feed," was the answer.

"Well, do you think you can keep a secret?"

"I've kept many of 'em."

"You say you have?"

"Yes, you know I have."

"Humph! Well, now we've another one for you to keep, and we don't want any damn foolishness about it. Here are our clothes. Take and wash them as soon as you can. Don't let father see them. And remember this, if we ever hear anything of this blood it will be at the cost of your life. A hint to the wise is sufficient. You understand us? We mean just what we say."

She promised and obeyed.

They were summoned to breakfast, and the old man, not seeing the stranger, asked what had become of him, at the same time remarking that his horse was not in the stable.

The question had been anticipated, and the answer was ready.

"He went to Mark Shain's. At least he said he was going there, and we showed him the way. We got near there, and being tired, concluded not to hunt any longer, as he said that he did not feel very well. We had told him a heap about Mark, and he seemed anxious to see him. He said, if we'd excuse him, he would go there and spend the night. But, I'll bet, Pink, he didn't find the way," said Dock.

Pinkney said, hesitantly, "Well, I don't know———"

"He got lost before he got to Mark's field fence," said Dock, interrupting.

"Whar hed you bin all night?" asked the old man. "You never got in until nearly day."

"O, we were browsing around. You oughtn't to ask so many questions," replied Dock.

The subject was dropped, but had the old man noticed the expression on the old lady's face, his suspicions would have been aroused, and the horrible truth ferreted out.

Another difficulty presented itself, for, as Dock ceased talking, the old man remarked, "Speak of the devil and his imp will appear. Good mornin', Mark."

"Yes, and by damn, just in time, too," said Mark Shain, as he leaned upon his old flint-lock in the door.

"Yes," responded the old man, "just in time. Hev a cha'r at the table. Ole lady, fix a plate thar."

"No, no; not for me," said Mark. "It's too early for dinner, and I've been to breakfast, thank you. I've something for these chaps," indicating Dock and Pinkney by an inclination of his head.

The boys started, glanced at each other, and one of them stammered, "What for?"

"O, it makes no difference. You've got to go, and that quick. Here's my dogs; you know them; and here's my gun. I think we can get a buck or two this morning, if we'll hurry up."

An expression of relief replaced that of the alarm on their countenances, which that worthy readily detected, and remarked that if he had known they were so easily frightened, he'd have spoken a little rougher.

"O no, not scared," said Dock hasitly, "but I was regretting that we could not go, as we have to get up some cattle today."

"I s'pose," said the old man, to Mark, "that you hed a stranger with you las' night. He come here, but I reckon he didn't like our fare and thought he'd try yours."

"Not a word of it so, sir," said Mark. "There's been no man at my house."

"What!" exclaimed the old man.

"What as much as you please. There's been no stranger at my house lately."

The old man looked keenly at the boys.

"We started to your house last night to have a fox chase," said Dock, "and the man who was with us had come to stay all night here, but when he got in your neighborhood we spoke of you to him and where you lived, and all. And he said he had heard of you and would like to see you. And then, complaining of feeling unwell, said he believed he would go and spend the night with you if we would excuse him, and that, perhaps, he would call by here this morning. So, you haven't seen him?"

"Not a bit of him. But that's off the subject, I reckon. I want to know whether or not you are going to take a drive with me?"

The boys persisted in thanks and excuses, and Shain, after muttering a few good humored dry damns, bade them good morning and disappeared among the hills.

The afternoon came, and the old man was taking his usual after-dinner nap when the boys slipped to the woods and Big Mouth with shelled oats and a spade. The dead body and mare were as they left them. The latter was fed, and the former removed from the crevice and buried near where it fell under the strokes of their cruel knives.

CHAPTER XXI. William Mayfield

There was a round of pistol shots heard in the woods near the Brown place—five reports—which was answered by Pinkney Brown with a single shot.

"What does that mean?" asked James House of the latter.

"O, nothing much. It's only Dock coming home," was the reply.

James House is a carpenter and resides at Caneyville, in this county. He was at work for the Browns at the time mentioned. He says that he stayed many months with them, and this signaling was an invariable custom with them. Five shots were fired by the returning party, and the answer was according to the surroundings. If the coast was clear, the reply was one shot; if not, or doubtful, two shots.

One night Dock was coming home. Some strangers had just alighted. Five reports were heard from Dock's pistol and Pinkney answered it with two. The strangers, from some cause, did not stay all night, and after they left, Pinkney fired a single shot, and Dock came in, just as he did on the evening referred to above. He was riding a black mare, which he had owned for some time, and leading Pugh's sorrel which he had taken from the cave. She had changed in appearance, having been in the cavern for several weeks. He had taken a drove of cattle to Louisville and returned by Big Mouth.

The family expressed much admiration for the sorrel mare and wanted to know where he had come across her and what she had cost him. All their questions were answered as had been previously arranged between him and Pinkney.

"Well, what luck?" asked the old man.

"Not very good," was the answer. "I lost three head and made a very small profit on the others. But I reckon I didn't lose anything."

The chores were done, and the brothers went to the spring. When the bucket was filled, Pinkney remarked:

"Dock, I reckon it is about time you were giving me my part of that nine hundred dollars. We divided the gold, and I think you have put me off long enough about the other."

"Yes, that's so," said Dock, "but to tell you the honest, God's truth, Pink, there were but six hundred dollars in the bills."

"Six hundred!" exclaimed Pinkney. "You know that is not so. Only six hundred besides the gold! Pshaw! Don't talk to me that way."

"I say there were only six hundred besides the gold. Only six hundred in bills. That's just what I said, and that's just what I meant."

"What's the use to tell a damned lie about it?" hotly responded Pinkney. "You know you are lying. Didn't we count the money before you took it?"

"Don't fly off the handle," expostulated Dock, "and I'll explain——"

"I don't want you to explain," interposed the other. "You can't explain. It explains itself."

"Just wait a minute. I thought there were nine hundred at the time, too, but when I counted it next day there were only six hundred. This is the God's truth. I didn't understand it at first—I thought I had lost three hundred. This is why I put off the division with you, thinking the three hundred might possibly turn up. But now I am satisfied there were only six hundred at the start, and the damned rascal beat us in the count for the purpose of swindling us out of three hundred dollars next morning. But we settled with him a little different from that, eh? And now, more than ever, do I feel that we did right in killing him, the damn son of a——"

Outlaw of Grayson County

"Come, now, Dock, it is not worth while to jest about this matter. The fair thing is the fair thing, and I want my money."

"Jest, the devil!" said Dock. "I'd like to know why you think I am jesting?"

"Well, I've my opinion," retorted Pinkney.

"What is your opinion?"

"O, it's unnecessary to name it."

"Well, by——! I say it is necessary to name it!"

"Pshaw! If you think I'm afraid, I'll just say that I always will believe that you are keeping the other three hundred."

Each man, now thoroughly angered, drew his pistol.

"Hold, Pink!" exclaimed Dock. "There's no use of our killing each other over as small an amount as one hundred and fifty dollars. That's all there is between us."

"That's all," said Pinkney, lowering his weapon. "And now you can give me my part, and the matter may drop."

"Here's one hundred, and there's fifty," said Dock, handing him the money. "It's a clear loss to me, but if you can live with it, I am sure I can live without it."

"I don't want any more than is honestly due me," said Pinkney.

"That's all right," said Dock.

"Then it's due me," responded the other.

"Well, you've got it, and you ought to be satisfied," was the reply. "And now I propose that hereafter we divide everything equally on the spot at the time it is made."

This was their agreement in regard to all future business transactions.

They herded several hundred head of cattle, sheep, hogs and other livestock on the old place and on the broad acres of the woodland adjoining. The cattle were generally kept in the woods during the summer when they grew fat on the wild pea vines which covered miles square of the forest until within the last twenty years. A few vines are still to be met with there but are rapidly being choked out by undergrowth which is produced by the foolish custom of annually burning the leaves. But for this our Kentucky forests would be as lovely as in the days of Boone and Kenton.

For a time the Browns were regarded as models of business and enterprise in Grayson. In fact, there were but few moneyed men within the circuit of their business who would not empty their purses to either upon the request of a loan. But at length a little cloud of suspicion arose amongst some of their neighbors.

DOCK BROWN

On one occasion, Pinkney and Dock had sent a large drove of fat cattle to Louisville by Mayfield. Pinkney had bought Dock's interest in them, and the former had advised Mayfield to deposit the proceeds of their sale in the Louisville Bank of Kentucky. This was done, and Mayfield returned home. Shortly afterward, Dock drove a number of hogs to the same market, and having learned of Mayfield's deposit in the bank, he got a man to identify him as a brother and partner of Pinkney Brown, and that they were stock men from Grayson, and he succeeded in drawing the five hundred dollars deposit by Mayfield.

He returned to Pine Knob but said nothing about the money. A few weeks thereafter, Pinkney gave a man with whom he had some dealings a check on the bank. It was dishonored, with the statement that P. H. Brown had drawn his whole deposit. Dock was at once suspected. Pinkney accosted him about it, and he apparently became very angry and remained so for several days.

When Pinkney acquainted Mayfield of his suspicions about Dock, the latter said: "There's no use in Gullie whining, for he has got the money and will have to fork it over."

When Dock returned from Caneyville, where he had gone on a trading expedition, the boys, with pistols presented, demanded the bank money, saying: "Hand it out, for we know you've got it."

"This is robbery!" protested Dock. "I've got that much, but not a cent of it belongs to anybody except myself. I'll let you have it, and all I have, rather than get into a difficulty with you. I never expected such treatment from my brothers."

"Well, you are the cause of it. You had no business taking money that was not yours. I'd be ashamed of this, Gullie," said Pinkney.

"I'll swear that I never got a cent out of the bank that was not mine!" said Dock.

"You may swear and be damned," was the reply, "but that is not the money. So hand it out or I'll shoot a hole through you!"

"Hold a minute!" cried Dock, "till I can get it out. Here, now, I'll give it to you, but don't say anything about it, for you know it would do none of us any good."

"We've not told anybody that you got it," said Pinkney, pocketing his money, "but why in hell don't you be honest and pack fair with me?"

"If you'll pack fair with me hereafter," replied Dock, "I'll pack fair with you."

Outlaw of Grayson County

Ned Deweese, who lived near Pine Knob, had a horse stolen. He had swapped for him with one William May, of Elizabethtown, only a few weeks before. Soon after the theft the animal was found loose in the woods. But a Mr. Milburn, from Meeting Creek, having heard of the horse, came to Deweese's and identified the horse as his. He said it was stolen from him; he had traced it to May, who bought it of a man who exactly suited the description of Dock Brown, who was suspected of both thefts but was not arrested.

This circumstance, however, had but little effect upon the community, owing to the suppression of talk by the Browns' intimate and influential friends. It was supposed that the Browns knew nothing of these suspicions entertained by some of their neighbors. But a leak had been sprung, and the dam that supported them was soon to burst asunder.

Mrs. Silas Mahurin, a near neighbor, paid an occasional visit to old lady Brown, and on one occasion when she came down to spend the day there, the door of the little room was open, and she discovered a couple of strange looking objects in there, which upon close examination she found to be a pair of shoes with fresh mud on them and with heels upon the toe ends. She had heard of the horse stealing, and she now put that and this together, formed an opinion, but said nothing for a time, except to her family, and its members preserved silence for the reason that they were afraid to talk; and for the further reason that they feared the incredulity of the Browns' many friends, and that any report they might circulate to their detriment would be frowned down and themselves branded as slanderers.

It is hard to shake the confidence of an honest, faithful friend. And I have doubts of its ever being entirely eradicated after reciprocal trust has once become thoroughly established.

About this time another Richmond man took up his abode at Pine Knob. His headquarters were at the Browns. He said that his name was William Mayfield and claimed to be from Virginia and half-brother to Pinkney and Dock. It was not long until he was assigned to a post of duty, but his business seemed to be more upon the outskirts than at home. He would frequently leave and remain away for weeks at a time. While at Browns' he assisted in the management of the livestock, but as he was said to be an illegitimate son of old man Brown's, he, for this reason, took a humbler position in society than our full-blooded heroes.

CHAPTER XXII. A Trip to New York

In February, eighteen hundred and forty-five, Dock left home with the avowed purpose of going to Tennessee on a pleasure trip. At least, such was the impression upon the minds of his friends. But the family knew his destination was Lexington, Kentucky, where he proposed to speculate in cattle. He traveled horseback and reached Lexington in a few days after leaving home.

Here he learned that Mr. Thomas Hughes, who lived a few miles from town, was a large trader in stock. He rode out to the Hughes residence. As he halted in the lane in front of the dwelling of the latter, three men, coming from the opposite direction, also rode up and halted by him. He asked for Mr. Hughes. That gentleman, being one of the trio, promptly responded that he was the man and invited Dock to alight.

"I believe I will, thank you," said Dock. "My name is Brown."

"Glad to meet you, Mr. Brown," said Hughes heartily. "Let me introduce you to Mr. White, also Mr. Wood."

The introduction was recognized by all parties, and they entered the house together.

Thomas Hughes was the father of the Hughes whose tragic death, and the equally tragic event immediately preceding it, some years later, rendered his name notorious in that portion of the state. He waylaid and killed his uncle, a gentleman named Smith, and immediately put an end to his life—the bodies of the murderer and his victim being found lying close together.

The White mentioned as one of the parties introduced to Dock, is Dr. G. W. White, at present a resident of Elizabethtown but at the time of the meeting with our hero he and Lewis Wood resided in Pulaski County, where the latter still lives.

Hughes had a fine drove of cattle, numbering one hundred and seven head, which Dock was anxious to buy, but the former refused all offers, and finally employed Dock, Wood and White to drive them to New York for him, Dock to have charge of them.

Upon the first evening of their journey they stopped to spend the night at the house of a widow. She was the mother of a charming daughter, also a widow, who was about nineteen. Here, thought Dock, is an opportunity to outshine the boys. But it was only an opportunity to display his natural effrontery and vanity, which were prominent traits in his character as well as any species of his well reputed rascality.

He affected to be greatly smitten with the young widow, whose

Outlaw of Grayson County

pleasantness and kindness to strangers, at her home, he misconstrued. He sought her as she was drawing water from the well and accosted her with:

"Let me assist you."

"No, thank you," she replied. "I can assist myself. I am used to work."

"You ought not to be," said Dock, as he lifted the bucket which hung full at the end of the ascending sweep-pole. "I'm opposed to women working, anyway; especially when they are as pretty as yourself."

Unacquainted with the world's deception, the pretty widow smiled complacently as Dock proposed to carry the bucket of water for her.

"I'm a single gentleman," said the audacious fellow, "and I want to get acquainted with you. I own the drove of cattle, and these others are only hired hands of mine. I own one hundred and fifty Negroes in Tennessee."

"See here , mister, I don't care for your Negroes. And if——"

"Well, I know, but—wait, just a minute. Say—oh—I'm coming back this way soon and visit you. I won't have these ruffians along with me then, and say——"

"Look here, mister," she interrupted, "if you want any supper tonight you had better take that water in the house, or let me have it, one or t'other."

"O, yes, certainly. I didn't mean to detain you. But, say, when I come back——"

Here he caught sight of Mr. White (who was sitting inside of the window and heard every word that he had said) and paused abruptly. The widow hurried into the kitchen with the pail of water.

Next day, on the road, he asked Dock why he had lied so to the young woman the evening before. The latter replied that he didn't mean any harm by it—that he only wanted to see what he could accomplish. "Besides," said he, "I wanted a little extra attention, and you see I got it, for they had but little to say to either of you."

"That's all right," said White, "but I want to know what you meant by calling Wood and me ruffians."

"I didn't do it," said Dock unblushingly. "You misunderstood me."

"There is no misunderstanding about it," asserted White. "You said it. I tell you that I heard every word you and that lady said."

DOCK BROWN

"Well," persisted Dock in denial, "you might have understood it that way, but I didn't say that. If I did it was not about either one of you. You know I've got nothing against you, and why should I talk so about you? It don't stand to reason, you see."

"You may squirm out of it that way if you want to," said White, "and also out of the lie you told about the stock and your Tennessee Negroes."

Here the cattle demanded the attention of both men, and the matter thus ended between them.

Before crossing the Ohio River they stayed all night at a Mr. Glenn's, and during the night the cattle broke into their host's hemp field, and as it was raining, each brute made his bed on a hemp shock, thus almost demolishing the man's entire crop of hemp. They were starting next morning without offering to pay any damage. Glenn broached the matter to Brown, but the latter replied that he would not pay a damned cent, for it was natural for stock to break bad fences, and if his fence had been of any account, they would not have got into his field.

"That is perhaps all true enough," said Glenn, "but I think it would be nothing but right to pay me something, as I was very moderate in my charges for feeding the cattle and charged you nothing for your meals and lodging."

"That was your own lookout, and not mine," was the brutal response.

"Pay him what is reasonable for the hemp," interposed White and Wood. "It is nothing but right."

"Here's a dime," said Dock. "Will that do?"

"Mr. Brown, you are no gentleman," indignantly exclaimed the insulted Mr. Glenn. "And now, sir, since you have shown it so plainly and have been so insulting, I intend to have full pay for my hemp or sell every hoof of cattle in that drove." Saying which, he turned away.

Dock, seeing that he meant to do exactly as much as he said, called to him to know how much he wanted.

"Only fifty dollars," was the response.

"I'll give you half of it," said Dock.

"No you won't," was Glenn's answer. "But I'll tell you what I will take, and not a cent less. And it is not worth while to multiply words about it."

"Well, how much?" asked Dock, as he pulled out his purse.

"Thirty-five dollars," said Glenn.

Outlaw of Grayson County

"There's the money," and Dock counted down the sum named. "And now that I've paid for the hemp, I am coming back by here to get it in a few days."

"Very well, sir," said Glenn. "I'll see you when you come, I hope."

Many similar compromises of petty matters were made by Dock on the trip, he coming out second best in most of his ranting audacity and dishonesty.

He and Wood had a difficulty about which one should go before the drove. Brown's language to Wood was very insulting, and but for the timely interference of White the latter would have killed him. Dock, discovering he was mistaken in the quality of mettle he had aroused, requested White to inform Wood that his services as a driver were no longer desired. White told him as requested, but Wood refused to quit, giving as his reason for remaining that he had been employed by Hughes and not by Brown, who was himself only a hireling. No further communication passed between the two on the trip except through White.

They crossed the Ohio at the mouth of Cabin Creek and pursued their route through Chillicothe, Ohio; Wheeling, Virginia; Cumberland, Maryland; Harrisburg, Pennsylvania, and thence to New York.

While in Pennsylvania they spent a night at the residence of another widow. There being no men about the place, she trusted them with the measurement of the corn and other feed. Dock requested of White that he and Wood should leave the management of this matter to him and that he would make something by the operation. Dock reported that he paid the widow next morning for a much less quantity of provender than was actually used.

A few weeks after, White and Wood, having left Dock in New York, returned to Hughes and acquainted him with Dock's general villainy, including the above robbery of the Pennsylvania widow. Hughes said that he wanted no one to steal for him and then, in a letter to the widow, inclosed her five dollars, which White informed him would amply pay her for the forage Brown had failed to report and pay for. Hughes then read them a letter he had received from Dock. The sentence that particularly interested them read as follows:

"If White and Wood should want you to pay them something for their work, don't do it; for I have paid them both off, and more too than they deserve. Wood is a scoundrel and a thief. I have learned that much about him. White is not much better. Wood tried to steal the money you gave me for expenses."

"Was there ever such a scoundrel as he is, upon the face of the earth?" exclaimed Wood.

"Never, I reckon," assented White.

"Did he pay you gentlemen?" asked Hughes.

"Not a cent in the world," was the response. "And there is not a word of truth in his letter."

The whole story about Dock was a plausible one. Hughes accepted their statements as facts, and became quite uneasy lest Dock should not return. He tendered the hospitality of his home to the two men, requesting them to remain a few days and await Brown's return. They accepted, and within a day or two Dock put in his appearance, greatly chagrined and disappointed at finding Wood and White there, having postponed his return, as he supposed, a sufficient time for them to have gone.

It was with difficulty that Wood was restrained from attacking him the moment he got sight of him. Wood and White remained in the house until Dock, who was met at the gate by Hughes, had alighted and entered the yard. They then came out and looked him square in the face, White saying:

"How are you?"

Dock barely looked up and, muttering an inaudible response, turned his attention to Hughes, who invited him to the house. Seated in the parlor, he asked him a few questions which Dock brazenly answered. The pressure was so great, however, that he was not long in drawing Dock's letter and asked him if he wrote it.

"Yes, by God!" was his reply, "and every word of it is as true as gospel!"

White and Wood sprang to their feet simultaneously and denounced him as a low flung, lying puppy and thief, and told him to take it back or they would cut his throat upon the spot.

"Hold, gentlemen! This won't do!" cried Hughes. "This is not the time or place to have a difficulty, and I will not allow it in my house. You promised me to keep quiet before he came, and I hope you will be as good as your word."

Brown had backed into a corner against the bed, with a pistol in one hand and a dirk in the other. His antagonists had nothing but pocket-knives. Hughes requested the latter to go into another room, stating that he would make an amicable settlement of the difficulty. They acceded to his request, but with reluctance.

"Now, Mr. Brown," said Hughes, "I want to know the truth about this matter, for I tell you, your life is in great danger. These men have every appearance of honesty, but your letter has made them desperate. A great deal depends upon what you now say. Is what you wrote about them true? Have you paid them anything?"

"Well, no. But Wood acted the damned rascal with me, and I didn't want him to have any pay. He don't deserve any, for he did more harm than good."

Hughes settled with Brown and requested him to leave and never come upon his premises again. Waiting until he had mounted and gone, Hughes entered the room where White and Wood were impatiently waiting, told them of Brown's acknowledgment and that he had sent him away. After paying them their full wages and discussing what manner of a man Brown was, the affair ended and was heard of no more.

Dock had told the young widow, upon his return to her house, that he had been robbed the night before of nearly all he had realized by the sale of the cattle. It was evidently his intention to make a similar statement to Hughes, but being detected in his letter falsehoods, he felt in his nonplus that further action in that direction would prove a failure.

When he left Hughes he returned to Pine Knob to tread the well-beaten paths of the past, with an onward look to fields of more extended breadth wherein to gratify his extended villainy. His satanic cunning and roughshod impudence at Pine Knob were mistaken (and consequently admired) by some for wit and careless independence, such is an advantage which real or reputed wealth always commands.

CHAPTER XXIII. Miss Emma Ross

It is an indisputable fact that in this country money and tongue have been, and will ever be, a passport to the first circles of society. And how frequently is this unmerited market value estimated as true worth! The young man who considers himself fortunate in the possession of both carries a weight of fearful responsibilities, whose magnitude is regulated by the character and extent of advantages he accepts. The greatest and, doubtless, the most available of these responsibilities is the character and happiness of women upon whom so largely depend the welfare and happiness of community and nation. Some of these young men live the brute life, with no recognition of duty to God or their fellowmen. Others display traces of humanity in their remorse over sins of commission. The two characters have brought deeper disgrace and greater ruin upon the religious, political and moral status of the progressive world than all the drunkenness and wars that have cursed and shaken enlightened Christendom. In affluence, there is influence; in influence, advantage, which can be used for good or evil at option. If for the latter, it is a sin of commission—belongs to earth—and robs her of many of her most precious jewels. The innumerable host of once pure and noble women, whose breathing shells now grope still lower and deeper into sinks of iniquity, misery and wretchedness, with inseparable threads of disgrace extending to every sympathetic relative, is a living record of its most baneful ravages. But if for the former, which in this connection is simple resistance to temptation, it has no record on earth, for the world by this is none the wiser. It is a happy secret in the breast of "God's noblest work," and has a divinity invisible to mortal eyes or ken but which shines with unfading luster on the pages of eternal reward above.

In the midst of the Brown boys' immediate female relatives, as well as amongst many of their other female associates, are still to be found many haggard marks of degradation and shame—the offspring of Dock and Pinkney Brown's brutal passions. Although, as has been stated, they were admitted into the best circles of society in their section of the country, there was growing something so mysterious in their bearing of late years, which, in connection with their inferior cast of refinement, precluded, to some extent, a lengthy course of friendship, love, or confidence among recent acquaintances in the circle of the truly cultivated and intellectual. So, for this reason, together with their already partially injured reputations, their circle of associates gradually grew less, and the brothers were finally narrowed to a rivalry in their mutual admiration for the quiet, unassuming and modest Miss Emma Ross, of Leitchfield, whose father kept the hotel.

Their attentions to this young lady seemed constant and devoted. She not only possessed rare personal charms, but it was generally understood that her father had money. She loved neither but rather liked both. Indeed she would have discarded them as suitors had her father given them no encouragement with the wish to retain them as friends. But the "Mayor," as he was universally designated, imagined the bulk of their money and highly estimated them as men of cash. The boys warmly pressed their suits for many months, but at length as it became evident that Pinkney was in her favor and Dock out, the latter withdrew and left his more fortunate brother, for the time being, master of the situation.

Outlaw of Grayson County

It is deemed proper in this connection to introduce Jake Brazier, a man as well known in Grayson County as any character of this story, and one who will be long remembered in this portion of Kentucky. He was born of pious parents near Cincinnati, Ohio, but shortly after his father's death he ran away from home, came to Grayson County while quite a boy, and for some years resided with his uncle, William Spurrier, a man of high morals, honesty and industry, and who endeavored to smother the wild dissipations of Jake and stimulate in him laudable ambitions. Having met the Browns, Jake became one of their admirers and finally an indispensable auxiliary as a cattle driver and social confidant. He was then about eighteen years old and spent most of his time in their company and employment, and yet he seldom remained at their house over night. This was because the boys had told him that their father had taken an unaccountable dislike to him and did not want him around after dark. Jake didn't care for this, as there were other places he could stay, and was not deprived of the boys' company.

In general matters he was confidant of both, but in their love affair with Miss Ross he was Dock's, to which he proved recreant, as he acquainted her with many things detrimental to his character, and when he learned that she was engaged to Pinkney he told her that she would never marry him.

"Why, Jake?" she inquired.

"I'm afraid to say," he replied.

"Afraid! Of what, pray tell me?"

"I won't say now, but you'll find out in time," was the tantalizing answer.

"But you must tell me," she persisted, "for you have excited my curiosity. There must be something wrong or you would not be afraid. Tell me now."

"I know Dock Brown," he said, hesitatingly, "and I think there is something in the wind. I don't know what it is, but he loves you himself, you know, and ———"

"Well, what if he does," she interrupted. "He knows that I don't love him. But, what were you going to say?"

"You won't say anything about it?"

"I won't speak of it," she assured him.

"Well, Dock told me that he intended to marry you. He said something about Pink, too, but I can't tell you that."

This and all other interviews with Brazier were stolen when the Mayor was out of town. On this occasion his return cut short the conversation as above. Miss Emma availed herself of every opportunity to converse with Brazier, for he always had something of interest to tell her whether true or false, but which she always accepted as true.

Pinkney informed Dock of his intended marriage, and the latter expressed himself in terms of great approbation and tendered his assistance, saying:

"It's a lucky hit, Pink, a lucky hit. I wanted her myself,y ou know, but of course it was for her money, and I suppose she found it out. But you know that is all either of us ever cared a damn for."

"No, you are mistaken," said Pinkney. "I love her, and intend to marry her for love alone."

CHAPTER XXIV.
Theft of the Weatherford Mare—An Investment in Slaves

The sorrel (or Pugh) mare was claimed by many to be the fleetest animal in Grayson County, being the only animal, it was said, "that could head a steer in a lane." This gave her some notoriety among the jolly Grayson County boys.

Dock rode her into Leitchfield once on a "big court day" and took her around on "Jockey Street." She being a much finer animal than was commonly seen on "Jockey," she attracted no little attention, and some one ventured the remark that she looked very much like the mare that a strange man rode through the town. Dock instantly thought of Pugh and quickly said that she never had been in Leitchfield before, as he had recently bought her in Louisville. Shortly afterward, fearing that others would also recognize her as being the animal Pugh had ridden and thus caused unpleasant surmises, if nothing more serious, to be bred in the community, Dock took her to Warrick County, Indiana, and sold her.

Here he unexpectedly met his brother, Jim, at whose house he remained for several days. Jim had also changed his name and, by a remarkable coincidence, had assumed that of Brown. There they were enabled to pass as brothers without any trouble, both bearing the same name. A few years before this Jim had lost his wife and was keeping house, his family consisting of his little boy and a hired cook.

Dock left Warrick afoot and returned home by way of Rockport, Stephensport and Hardinsburg. At the latter place he loitered about for a day or more and finally left unceremoniously one night, forgetting to pay his hotel bill. He went out a few miles into the country to William Weatherford's, slipped into that gentleman's stable and stole his roan mare, which he hurriedly rode to his home in Grayson.

Early next morning after his theft, Mark Shain and Frank Porter were coon hunting in the vicinity of Pine Knob, and while Shain was absent at his house, where he had gone to procure an ax to fell a coon tree, Porter heard the trampling of a horse's feet in the road above. He called out to learn who it was. The rider did not answer but instantly struck out into a rapid gait in an opposite direction from the one in which he seemed to have been traveling.

On the return of Shain, Porter informed him of the circumstance, which had somewhat excited his curiosity, but they felled the tree, which awoke the sleeping echoes of the hills with its crash, and the coon racked only a few paces before Tige overhauled him, and then the men enjoyed for several minutes an old-fashioned conflict between dog and raccoon, resulting, of course, in the triumph of the former.

Shain and Porter then left the hollow and ascended the hill to the road where the latter had heard the horse, and followed the tracks a short distance, when Shain turned back and went home; but Porter followed the trail until it led him into Big Mouth. The tracks were fresh, and he entered the cave a short distance until he satisfied himself that they did not return. Suddenly realizing his jeopardy, he hastily retreated and went to Shain's and acquainted him with the facts. This was Porter's first intimation of the existence of Big Mouth.

The two men immediately proceeded to Haynes's store, three miles distant, and got Henry Haynes, Gallatin Porter, Elisha Peyton and J. Y. Tilford, and the six, all well armed, went directly to the cave, but only to find that the horse had come out. They examined the cave for some distance and then came out and followed the returning tracks to the Cloverport and Bowling Green road. It was then dark, and they dispersed for their several homes.

Dock Brown and the Weatherford mare were in the cave when Porter came there, and it was, perhaps, well for the latter that he penetrated no farther than he did, for Dock was only about sixty yards from the entrance, where, invisible himself in the darkness, he could distinctly see Porter's every movement.

That night Dock fired the usual signal shot for Pinkney to meet him in the woods. The latter responded promptly, and in a little while Dock, with a scanty supply of edibles, was on his way to Tennessee. He arrived at the residence of John S. Byas, the husband of his sister, Polly, swapped the mare to him for a mule and, riding it, reached Pine Knob in two days, having made the round trip of two hundred and fifty miles in three days and a half. He arrived at home on Saturday, and the next day went to the blacksmith shop of J. Y. Tilford to have the mule shod. As the day was Sunday, Tilford refused to do the work. Dock, after giving full vent of his spleen by curses and threats, was permitted to shoe the animal himself.

Before closing this chapter it may be well to mention the fact that in the year eighteen hundred and forty-three Dock and Pinkney purchased two colored girls of one Anselm Watkins, near Falls of Rough. They paid five hundred dollars for Letitia and four hundred for Lucy, cash in hand. They subsequently bought two Negro boys, Ambrose and Sam, and built a cabin in the yard for their occupation. The girls did most of the cooking and all of the sewing for the family. In eighteen hundred and forty-six they were pretty well grown and thoroughly trained to do the will and obey the commands of their young masters. Lucy made their pantaloons with private pockets along the leg seems and waistbands, for the concealment of small saws and other jail-breaking implements.

CHAPTER XXV.
Murder of Their Brother James and Son by the Browns

Evan Rogers, of Leitchfield, sold and delivered to the Browns at Pine Knob twenty-two head of cattle. It being nearly dark when he was ready to start home, the boys invited him to spend the night with them. He politely declined, stating that the nights were pleasant and he could easily ride home. But the Browns importuned him so earnestly and seemed so hurt at the idea of his leaving their home at such an hour that he finally agreed to stay. After supper they proposed to pay him for the cattle, but Rogers told them that they could pay him in the morning as well. Dock insisted, saying that he didn't want to go to bed owing anybody. They counted it out and handed it to him. Rogers was assigned the little room for the night. "But," says he, "I didn't sleep a wink. I drew the bed across the door and sat up all night in misery."

Next morning his and Dock's horses were saddled, the latter proposing to ride over the hill with him and show him Big Mouth. They started toward their horses, but Pinkney called Dock back and they carried on a whispered conversation for a minute or two. Rogers was at the gate only a short distance from them but could not hear a word that was said except when they were separating, he heard Pinkney say, "That won't do, I tell you in earnest."

This aroused Rogers's suspicions. They rode off on the Leitchfield road a short distance and then turned off for the cave, Rogers in the rear, all the time watching for an opportunity to dodge. He followed slowly on the ridge until near the cave. When Dock reached the brow over Big Mouth, he called to Rogers to come. "All right!" the latter responded. Dock rode around and went down. The instant he was out of sight, Rogers turned his horse and, at full speed, started for home. Dock called for him, but receiving no answer, come out and hollered to him to come back, assuring him that he would not hurt him. But Rogers did not return.

Some time afterward they met in Leitchfield, and Dock asked Rogers why he got scared. The latter told him that he didn't like his maneuvers with Pinkney before they started. "Besides," he said, "I saw no sense in going down to that old cave."

Dock laughed and endeavored to remove the impression he could not fail to see that his former action had made upon Rogers, but the latter walked away from him, at the some time telling Dock not to come near him in the future. At this Dock fired up and angrily said:

"You can go to hell!"

"So can you," retorted Rogers, "and you will go there. And just now keep your carcass out of my way and I'll not interrupt you."

"That's a bargain," said Dock.

"Yes," said a voice near.

Dock wheeled around, and there upon a horse, sat his brother Jim. They shook hands, passed a few words, Dock mounted his horse, and they left together for the Knob. During their ride Dock asked him if he had told anybody in this county his name. Jim replied that he had; that he had called himself Brown ever since he left home, and had claimed to be a brother to the Brown boys in Grayson; that he had heard them spoken of so favorably by many that he was glad to claim relationship.

The old man gave James a warm welcome, but after he had spent several days there it was found that he had but little money, and then there was a manifest desire to have him leave. But he took no hints. In a private conversation he asked his father how Pinkney and Dock got hold of so much property, and if the most of it did not belong to him. The latter said that he had some property, but the most of everything belonged to Pinkney and Dock, and that he had not meddled himself to the extent of trying to find out how they made it. He then asked Jim why he wanted to know so much about the property.

"Because," said Jim, "I think it is yours, and that I have as good a right to some of it as Pink and Gullie."

"Well," said the old man, "you are not very apt to get any o' mine. Not yit, nohow."

Jim, seeing that he had stirred up the old man's ire, dropped the subject and left his presence. The boys had suspected his design in coming to Grayson, and tried to devise means of getting rid of him. They knew that he and the old man had had several private conversations, and they demanded of the old lady to know what they were about. She had learned the purport of the latter conference and, in substance, disclosed it to them. They exchanged

Outlaw of Grayson County

looks which said as plainly as spoken words: "Death—the grave—he shall die."

"How will we manage the thing?" asked Pinkney.

"The cave, of course," answered Dock.

"No, no; that'll never do," said the former. "He's too sharp to ever go there. You know that we've already treated him coolly, and he's not apt to give us a chance at him unless we get on the good side of him."

"That's the very thing," responded Dock, "if we only work it right. We can gradually get in with him, and then we've got him. He has already shown that it is his intention to stay till he is driven off. He don't pay no attention to what the old man says."

It was but a week after that they were to all appearance upon the best of terms. One day Dock proposed a partnership in stock trading, he and Pinkney to put in capital against James's labor; and also suggested that the latter go to Indiana, get his boy, bring him there, and they would all live together. James was much pleased and agreed to the proposition.

"But," said he, "what will I do with my little farm over there?"

"I hadn't thought of that," said Dock. "But if it will suit you we'll buy it and put the money in as capital in our partnership."

"That's all right," said James. "I'm in for anything just so you don't act the rascal with me." Then, laughing, he continued, "You know you and Pink are hard ones. I know you of old."

Dock smiled in turn and said, "Yes; I reckon you haven't forgotten Willis Roberts?"

"Pshaw! Let's hush talking so much," said James hurriedly. "When can we go to Indiana? I want one of you to go with me."

A few days after Jim and Dock arrived at Booneville, Warrick County. A deed of conveyance was made by James Brown to Pinkney H. and Gulliam Brown for the former's real property. The personalty had been disposed of before James came to Kentucky. They then called at a neighbor's house and, getting the little boy, started for Pine Knob.

They came by Cloverport, and proceeded directly to Uncle Jimmy Howard's where they arrived about ten o'clock in the morning, and remained until a short time after sundown. Jim had insisted upon leaving earlier, but Dock detained him on a pretense of trying to buy some stock of Uncle Jimmy. Finally they started as above mentioned, a little before sundown. Reaching the Falls of Rough, they started in the direction of Pine Knob, distant four miles, taking the road leading by Frank Landrum's. It was pitch dark, and

DOCK BROWN

Dock soon pretended to be lost. He told Jim that he had never before traveled that road from the Falls, but had frequently heard it said that it was much the nearest way they could go, and that was the reason he took it.

"But," said he, "I know now that we have missed the right road. We ought to have turned to the left more than a mile back. I know the woods and can cut off at least two miles by taking them. What do you say?"

"It makes no difference to me," replied James, "only Harry is sleepy and I want to put him to bed as soon as I can. I guess, though, we can make it through the woods. Harry, are you asleep?" The boy answered that he was not. "Well, look sharp now, or the brush will scratch you off. We are going through the woods."

On and on they went, over rocks and hills and through a forest dark as a dungeon, save now and then they were enabled to see about them by a flash of lightning from heavy clouds in the southwest, which rolled nearer and nearer as Dock led on toward the cruel and inhuman deeds so soon to be consummated by two as heartless and bloodthirsty villains as ever breathed the breath of life.

They reached the branch at the foot of the hill, whose clear but unconscious waters had once before aided the murders by cleansing their hands of the blood of poor Pugh. Dock was some twenty feet in advance, talking very loudly. Just then they passed a large moss-covered rock, which years before had broken loose from the cliff and rolled down to its present bed. Behind it Dock's alert ear caught the click of a gun-lock, which was speedily followed by a blinding flash and the deafening report of a musket. Jim's horse sprang forward and to one side, throwing him and the boy, the latter upon the roots of a tree and the former heavily upon him with a bullet wound in his shoulder. But with the instinct of self-preservation he speedily leaped to his feet, realizing that he had crushed his boy to death, but determined to sell his own life as dearly as possible. He rushed to the rock, calling upon Gullie to come back and help him kill the murdering scoundrel.

Dock's horse had been frightened by the shot, but he managed to leap from the animal's back and reached the rock before Jim. A flash of lightning disclosed to the latter the countenance of his two brothers. Dock had lost his pistol in jumping from his horse, and he now stood with his knife in his hand, and Pinkney with his gun, clutched by the barrel, ready to use it like a club.

"O! my dear brothers!" cried the horrified James, "don't kill me!

Outlaw of Grayson County

You've already killed my boy! You may have everything I've got! Pray let me live! I'll do anything—everything—for you, only let me———."

The unnatural pair had advanced upon him. Pinkney struck at him with his clubbed gun, but missed him and fell. Jim grasped the gun and was wrenching it from his hands when Dock plunged his knife in the poor fellow's side. Jim groaned and fell near his dying child. Another thrust with the knife and stroke with the gun, and the rain, which at that moment began to fall in torrents, washed the ghastly wounds in the body stilled forever in death.

Harry rolled over against Pinkney's feet, and deliriously murmured "Pa, I'm not hurt much. I'll get well."

"I think it's no use to do anything with him," responded Dock. "He's already about done."

As he spoke he knelt down by the child, placed his hand firmly upon its mouth, and held it there until its death struggles were ended.

The storm was still raging with unabated fury, and the murderers sought shelter in Big Mouth. Before entering they heard their horses neigh. They also had sought shelter in the cave and seemed glad at their masters' approach.

"We are in luck tonight," said Dock.

"Yes," said Pinkney. "But tell me why you didn't come last night. I stayed out here until twelve o'clock waiting for you."

"We couldn't get away from Hoosier any sooner," was Dock's reply. "Jim was about to get the gun away from you, wasn't he?"

"Yes, with only one hand, too; but you saved me. Good God! what is that?"

"Nothing but that same damned owl that scared Pugh to death," said Dock. "Wait till I get a rock, and I bet that I'll stop that winking."

Whiz-z-ip! and the stone rattled against the wall near the bird, bounded on, and fell with a dull splash in a dark pool of water beyond. The ominous eyes were invisible for a moment and then a snapping of beak and whirring of wings, and the yellow eyes glared upon them from another perch.

Dock attempted to find another stone to hurl at it, but desisted when Pinkney said:

"Let him alone. We've done enough killing for tonight, and we'd better be down there seeing about it."

They went home, procured the implements for digging, returned and buried the bodies of their victims in one grave by the side of Pugh.

CHAPTER XXVI. The Murder of Pinkney by Dock

In the fall of eighteen hundred and forty-seven Dock paid his mother and family (who still resided in Tennessee) a visit, remaining with them until the succeeding January. Upon his return home he discovered that he was not greeted by all of his friends with the expected and usual courtesies. But inasmuch as the Stinsons, Thomases, Cunninghams, and a few other moneyed families seemed still to be his friends, he cared but little for others. Evan Rogers had kept silent in regard to his adventure except to a few discreet friends, and did not make public mention of it until other developments justified publicity. He then spoke of the many letters that had come to his office, with strange superscriptions, and that were taken out by the Browns, who represented that the parties addressed were visiting their house.

Strangers did visit them, as well as many members of their own clan; but the fact that men were missing, and strange horses often seen in their possession, and the further fact that a great number of human skulls and other bones have been found in the neighboring caves and under the soil of the cellar to their dwelling, will warrant the belief that many who came to Pine Knob in that day never left.

On the morning of the thirty-first of January, eighteen hundred and forty-eight, the Brown family breakfasted by candle-light. Forty head of fat cattle, the joint property of the Brown boys, were ready for the road. Dock, Jake Brazier and some hired hands were starting with them that morning for Louisville.

Pinkney for several weeks past had been in delicate health, and Dock, who never practiced out of the family, was his physician. He had had given him frequent doses of calomel, which in those days was considered the panacea for all the ills that flesh is heir to.

As Dock was now about to leave for an absence of a week or more, he took from his pocket a small bottle containing six grains of corrosive sublimate and, dosing it into three powders, said: "Here, brother Pinkney, is a new sort of medicine. I find that calomel has done you no good. It has been too strong for your constitution. This is innocent and will have a tendency to brace you up. Take one of these powders every four hours, and if you are no better after you shall have taken them all, I advise you to send for Dr. Heston."

"When shall I begin?" asked Pinkney.

"Well, you may consume one powder about ten this morning. I'll leave the other doses on the table in the little room."

Outlaw of Grayson County

He gave Pinkney one powder and, after entering the little room, put the remaining two into a pint bottle of brandy which he then thrust into his pocket. Brazier and the others had already started with the cattle. Dock came out, invited Pinkney to go a short distance up the road with him, as a little exercise would do him good. They walked along, Dock leading his horse until out of sight of the house when, halting, Dock said:

"Well, brother, this, I guess, is as far as you ought to go. And now, as I leave you in bad health, it is possible that I may never see you again, and I want us to have a parting dram."

Pinkney took the bottle, saying: "Here's hope for the better; good luck to both of us, and with the cattle."

"The same, brother, but especially good health to you, and the hope that when I return I may find you sound and well," and he turned the bottle to his lips and pretended to indulge but exercising good care to not let a drop enter his lips. He made a wry face, as though the liquor was extra strong, extended his hand to Pinkney, saying, "Farewell," mounted his horse and rode away.

Pinkney watched the horse and rider until they were out of sight and then, feeling somewhat stimulated and a little better, went to the stable to see after his fine stallion. But he soon became very ill and went to the house and reclined upon the bed. He rapidly grew worse, with pains in his stomach, succeeded by cramping, nausea and vomiting. His father and the old lady were his attentive nurses. They inquired if Dock had left any medicine for him. He replied that there was a dose of medicine in his vest and told them to give it to him. They did so, and the pains and other symptoms grew worse. Dr. R. L. Heston of Leitchfield was sent for and arrived in the night. His diagnosis was that the man was laboring under the effects of poison. Then administering the antidotes at his command, expressed the opinion that there was little hope for his recovery. The patient steadily grew worse, and about nine a.m. the next day, after a convulsive tremor of intense suffering, his lips quivered, and audibly murmuring, "Come back, Gullie!" the crime-burdened and blood-stained soul of the man fled its casket and was stranded upon the gloomy brink of the unknown Beyond.

Dock returned within a few days and as he passed through Leitchfield held a handkerchief over his face, affecting sore affliction over his brother's death. He went home and then repaired alone to the grave on the hill. Not with the step of a grief-stricken brother but with hasty strides, as though to satisfy himself beyond doubt that his brother was dead and out of the way.

A few days after this, old man Brown called Isaac Deweese into his house to count some money. He brought out Pinkney's old fur cap, which contained over five hundred dollars in bank notes. After Deweese had counted it, the old man said:

"This an' some silver is what Dock give me for my intrust in Pink's estate. It'll run me an' the old 'oman our life-time, an' when we're gone he can lick the dish, for he's the only lawful heir."

The tone and manner of this declaration indicated something to Deweese beyond the ordinary meaning of words. He had heard that the old man suspected Dock of having murdered Pinkney, and that he entertained fears of a similar fate for himself, which led him to conclude that Dock had coerced the old man to make the foregoing statement to serve his purpose in the future. And the facts and circumstances that followed fully confirmed the correctness of Deweese's conclusion.

Dock loitered about the premises, apparently inconsolably wracked with grief over Pinkney's untimely death, soliciting and receiving by his silence and seclusion from society the condolence of a few unsuspecting and sympathetic friends.

But few weeks passed until he was again a frequenter of his old haunts, a wealthier and, possibly for that reason, a happier man.

Another difficulty, however, was upon him. William Mayfield, who had been in Tennessee for several months, came back and indicated an intention of making his home with the Browns. This was not all congenial with Dock's arrangements or wishes. Upon this, however, he kept silent, and for the purpose of ascertaining the amount of money in Mayfield's possession, proposed a partnership in general trade to the latter who had but a small yet sufficient amount for Dock's purposes. He was taken in as a partner, and not long thereafter they both started south with a drove of mules. That was the last ever seen or heard of Mayfield by any one in this county. Dock, on his return, told certain parties that they had lost on their stock, dissolved the partnership, and that Mayfield was at his home in Tennessee. Some believed him while others entertained a different opinion. As it is our purpose in this story to state nothing as a fact without at least circumstantial proof, we can only assert that it is a general and justifiable presumption that William Mayfield died on that trip under the fratricidal hand of his brother, for he was none other than William M. Hopper an own brother to Dock Brown.

CHAPTER XXVII. Dock Murders His Father

"I tell you, Jake, he won't do. No, sir; no, sir, he won't do at all. Did you ever notice that wolf eye of his? You know that Uncle Mark says a man can never shine a wolf's eye, and no man has ever shined Dock Brown's!"

Such was the exclamation of Dr. N. C. Tilford to Jacob Day as the two, in company with William Stinson, were riding to Leitchfield shortly after the death of Pinkney Brown.

"No," said Jake. "I'm like you, Doctor. I have no confidence whatever in the man and never had."

"Gentlemen," said Stinson, "I differ with you. I am better acquainted with Brown than either of you and know him to be an honest man."

"He may be," said one of the others, "but I can't consider him a safe and fair man in his dealings."

"Your lack of confidence," said Stinson, "arises from a very limited intercourse with him. There is no mistake that Dock Brown is most unjustly and very wrongfully persecuted. Some have gone so far as to say that they believed he poisoned Pinkney; that he has stolen horses; done a thousand other criminal acts. All of these assertions are vile calumnies, without even the remotest or skeleton of a foundation. From what Dock has said to me I am fully satisfied that he takes his brother's death very hard. The man has my deepest sympathy, for he seemed much affected a few days ago when he informed me that he had heard of the many reports about him. He said he paid little attention to most of them, but the one that he was suspected of killing his brother was too painful for patient endurance. I suppose that you have heard that he is soon to be married?"

"To Miss Ross?" asked Day.

"Yes," replied Stinson.

"Yes," said Tilford, "I suppose the whole country has heard of that affair. And right here let me tell you that this engagement with Ross's daughter has something to do in forming some of the opinions that he killed Pink."

"Because Pink was engaged to her?" queried Stinson.

"That's it," assented Tilford.

"Yes," exclaimed Stinson, "that's a fair sample of the kind of justice and charity meted out in heavy doses to the unfortunate man. Were similar circumstances to attend you, Doctor, or any other prominent citizen of the county, nothing would be suspected; but it is a fearful thing to be a stranger."

"As to the report, Uncle Billy, I have only spoken what I have heard," replied Tilford. "But I can tell you further that old man Brown himself suspects Dock of having killed Pinkney, for he told me so no longer ago than Tuesday when I was called to see Ambrose."

The conversation ended as they alighted in front of the Ross Hotel, and Uncle Pat took charge of their horses. The Mayor met them upon the porch and invited them to the public room where thirsty appetites were soon satisfied by the excellent refreshments from an old-fashioned English sideboard, which made the men realize, as they had often before, the truth that Ross's was the best hotel in Kentucky, notwithstanding the resemblance of the building to some antique, lightning-struck castle with which limners always picture the banks of the classic Rhine.

They were comfortably seated around the fire, engaged in lively conversation, when the parlor door opened and Dock Brown advanced with smiling face and graceful bearing.

"Uncle Billy, Doctor, Mr. Day, gentlemen, how do you all do?" was his suave salutation. "This is quite an unexpected pleasure. How did it happen that my three particular friends should be here together? I am glad to see you."

It matters not how justly a man's acts may deserve and receive both public and private censure, his appearance among a group wherein disparaging remarks have just been made regarding him will cause the speaker to experience feelings of discomfort. And in social intercourse there is no infringement upon the domain of conscience so easily and carelessly affected as backbiting, and few which inflict upon the conscience of an honest man deeper and more painful lashes.

Tilford and Day were correct in their opinion of Brown, but the affability of the latter caused them to regret having spoken of him as they did. Just censure and pure criticism should never have a motive to injure the sinning of faulty, but rather to condemn the sin and remedy the fault. What is spoken should never be spoken.

Dock had successfully pressed his suit with Miss Ross and bade her an affectionate adieu before entering the public room. He was now ready to return home. Stinson asked him to wait for company, but, strange to say, he declined and was soon riding along the highway toward the Knob.

Outlaw of Grayson County

Many were the speculations abroad relative to Dock's moneyed worth, and some asked others if it were really so that his own mother and brothers lived in Tennessee. For such was the general rumor floating incoherently among the people; but the facts were badly perverted before they were traced to a private letter received by one of Dock's friends. The letter simply made an inquiry about the Brown family, what they were worth and what doing. The letter was from Nancy and Ab Hopper, who claimed to be the mother and brother of Dock. It requested secrecy, but Dock saw it and was allowed to dictate an answer which mentioned Pinkney's unexpected death (?) and the old man's ill health, and the many pecuniary reverses the family had recently sustained.

Dock was made uneasy by the tone of the letter, for it indicated mercenary motives. He now purposed the immediate reduction of Pinkney's property to cash, the death of the old man, disposition of the old lady, a general sell out, and then the exit of himself to other parts of the country.

"But," said he to himself, "there is Miss Ross. I must marry her first, then my designs can easily be accomplished. What money she has will then be Dock Brown's. No, no; she can never live with father and the old lady. They must be put out of the way. I'd get nothing by killing the old lady, but when father's out of the way, I'm the only lawful heir. He said so himself in the presence of a witness who will stick to the track, and that is enough."

Thus he soliloquized as he sat in the little room on the evening of the twenty-first of May, eighteen hundred and forty-eight. The three were the only inmates of the house. The day's work was over. Dim twilight from a cloudless sky was fast falling. The innumerable voices in the near wildwoods, with which nature holds secret converse with the appreciative heart, fell dead upon the ears of this unhappy family. The old people sat in pensive silence near the eastern doorway. The night was unseasonably warm. Dock reclined upon his bed in the little room; by his side were his loaded pistols and gun. After all had retired, and the old lady and the Negroes were soundly slumbering, and even the watchdog had ceased his night howl all dismal in the secluded haunts of the forest home, Dock, hearing his father stirring, sleepless on account of the oppressive heat, called to him to come in there a while. He came, clad only in his night dress.

Dock told the old man that he would not be at all surprised to see Ab and Moses at any time, and that if they did come, somebody would have to die.

"I believe," said he, "that they are apt to come to that window you are sitting in and try to murder me in my sleep. If they do, I'll just lift my gun in this way," suiting the words to action, "and———." Bang! an instant after that two other shots followed in swift succession. The first shot was from the rifle, and took effect in the old man's head just above the ear, and he fell from the window, dead, upon the ground outside. The other two shots were from a pistol, also fired by Dock, and took effect in the wall behind his bed. (Some one has chipped the bullets out, but their prints are still there.)

The neighbors were summoned and came to the Brown place early next morning. The dead body of the old man was still under the window. An empty pistol was near it. The circumstance as detailed above form a sequence to the story Dock told.

"I was asleep," he said, "in my room. Some noise awoke me. I instantly arose and saw some one in the window. I reached for my gun which stood at the head of the bed. As I did so, two shots were fired at me. I then fired, and to my horror, a few moments afterward we found that I had killed my father!"

He then showed the bullet holes in the wall and continued: "You have heard all the threats that have been made against me, and so I supposed that some one had come to murder me—and O! it was my own father! I never dreamed of his having anything against me!"

The old lady was forced by Dock to corroborate his story by stating that the old man had gone to the window with his pistol for the purpose of assassinating him. The few remaining friends of the latter accepted these explanations as facts and regarded the affair as a sad misadventure.

The old man was buried on the hill by the side of Pinkney, and their graves are the ones mentioned in the introductory chapter of this story.

> They sleep the sleep their lives had won;
> Forever hidden, they must slumber on.

Dock surrendered himself into custody, but was acquitted of all guilt by a court of inquiry. He went home; gathered up all of the old man's and Pinkney's notes, accounts and money; forged assignment to himself of the former and pocketed the latter. Then, in order to exhibit honesty, called upon some of the most influential creditors of the deceased and paid off the small debts. With others he had difficulties and contentions too numerous to mention.

One other perplexing question he deemed must be solved before he could say, "Soul, take thine ease!" It was the disposition of the old lady before his marriage. At length he concluded to ship her to parts unknown. When she heard Dock's intention, she accepted and asked to be sent back to Virginia. She was soon placed in charge of a gentleman who was on his way to Louisville to purchase a fresh stock of dry goods. She reached that city, having fifty dollars in money and a rawhide trunk filled with clothing.

CHAPTER XXVIII
The Weatherford Mare—Unwelcome Visitors

David Weatherford, of Breckinridge, hearing that his mare had been seen in Grayson County, went to the Falls of Rough to make inquiries. There he met Jake Brazier, and knowing nothing about the man, asked him if he was "acquainted with one Dock Brown, who lived near Pine Knob." Brazier told him that he knew nothing about the mare, but as to Dock Brown, he knew him well.

"I suppose he is a clever man?" said Weatherford, as a feeler.

"Yes, sir," responded Jake, "of course, he is a clever man. Don't you know him?"

"I have no personal asquaintance with him," replied Weatherford, "but I have often heard of him."

"If you would like to see him," said Jake, "I'll go over to his house with you. He lives only eight or nine miles from here."

"No, thank you," hurriedly responded the other. "I don't wish to see him just now."

Weatherford had heard too much of Brown to be thus ushered into his presence at the solicitation of a man of Brazier's appearance. He turned away.

Notwithstanding Brazier's intimacy with Dock, he was ignorant of this theft. Now he understood all, and immediately went to Pine Knob and informed Dock of his meeting with Weatherford and of the interview between them.

"Who was with him?" asked Dock.

"I don't know," was the reply, "I saw another stranger there, but I don't know who he was."

"Did they leave before you?"

"No, I left them at the mill talking to Willis Green."

"Well, now, Jake, you must do some nice work for me," said Dock, "and do it quick. Keep an eye on Weatherford's movements and report to me. Will you do it?"

"You know I will," replied Jake. "You want me to go back to the Falls?"

"Yes, and follow them up," said Dock.

Weatherford and Jackson Wilkerson left the Falls and went up the Bowling Green road six miles to Haynes's store. Brazier followed them and found them in the store engaged in close conversation with several men. They were talking about the mare, but when Brazier entered, the conversation abruptly ceased. Clearly he was disturbed. But he heard a few disconnected remarks in which occurred the names of John Byas and Tennessee. He did not understand what these names meant but he remembered and reported them to one who did.

By daylight next morning Dock was fully seventy miles from home, rapidly traveling in the direction of Tennessee, his destination being John Byas's. During the succeeding night he reached the farm of the latter. The roan mare was in a pasture, where Dock quickly discovered her. He caught and led her into the woods, placed the muzzle of his pistol in her ear and fired. The animal fell dead at his feet. Dock then speedily skinned her and built a fire and burned the hide. He also cut off her feet and threw them into a sinkhole. Then he mounted his horse and returned home before he was missed from the neighborhood.

Weatherford proceeded to Tennessee in search of his mare and arrived at the house of Byas who did not hesitate to put him in possession of all circumstances connected with the acquisition of the mare. They were both satisfied that the slaughtered animal was the missing Weatherford mare, and that Dock had stolen it, but who did the killing was a mystery. Byas suspected Dock, but Weatherford repelled the suspicion as unjust because he knew (or thought he knew) that Dock was at his home at the time. He returned to Grayson County and there learned that Dock had not been away from home long enough to have gone to Tennessee and return. He then went to his home in Breckinridge County, and the matter was dropped for a time.

In the meantime, Dock continued his visits to Miss Ross. Those who strongly suspected him of crime feared him, and consequently never ventured to breathe their suspicions to the young lady or others of his friends and associates. He always went armed with

Outlaw of Grayson County

a brace of pistols, and no one doubted his willingness to use them upon his enemies whenever an opportunity for sure advantage should present itself. Men trembled from their own thoughts of heinous crimes and reckless bearing. He had become the special theme of conversation in many private circles, but of this fact he was ignorant, hearing nothing save an occasional, confidentially-ventured revelation made by some poor fellow in order to forestall the effect of his own backbiting in the event another should tell him.

Dock went to Louisville, bought monuments, and placed them at his father's and Pinkney's graves.

Shortly after this, Nathan Frizzle and Moses Hopper came to Pine Knob. When they arrived they found Dock at the spring house talking to Moses Edwards. The men had alighted at the gate yard when Dock first saw them. He and Edwards approached and spoke to them. There was an instant recognition, but nothing was said to disclose their relationship.

Moses, looking at Dock, said, "I wish to see you privately." They walked off to one side, and Edwards, receiving no attention from any of them, left.

"Who is that man, Gullie?" asked Moses.

"Well, sir, his name is—but, first, tell me why you ask?"

"I asked just to find out who he was. There is something familiar in his look. Don't you think he looks like father?" said Moses.

"That's what I expected you to say," said Dock. "But, come, let's go to the house. I want to hear from home before I talk about that. Moses, there's Letitia."

The mulatto was standing in her cabin door looking at the strangers.

"And that's Tish, is it? She's a good-looking gal."

"Yes," said Dock, "and the smartest nigger in the state. I wouldn't take a thousand dollars cash for her."

"Tell me now who was that man?" said Moses.

"I had thought of telling you to yourself, but Frizzle is in the family and it makes no difference. That man, sir, is your uncle," replied Dock.

"Who?"

"Why didn't you say so when he was here?" asked Moses.

"He goes by the name of Edwards," said Dock, "and nobody here knows him by any other name. You know all about why he changed his name, don't you?"

"Yes, I have heard," assented Moses.

Frizzle said he had heard his wife speak of her Uncle Moses, but he had never learned where he was, nor anything else much concerning him.

"He and father got into the same kind of scrape," said Dock, "and they changed their names. That's all."

After talking for some time over family matters, Moses and Frizzle told Dock that they had come for the purpose of paying him a short visit and perhaps would buy him out if he would sell.

Dock perfectly understood their deception and offered them his entire possessions at about one-fourth their value. He knew they would not accept, and his proposition was only a disguised intimation that he suspected them of having no notion to buy, but of having come there as spies interested in the amount of property he had.

"How much of this belonged to father and Pink?" asked Moses.

"None of it," replied Dock. "Pink owed me several hundred dollars, and a short time before he died assigned to me all of his property in order to secure me. I have paid his debts with some of it. And father also assigned his share to me and Pink for taking care of him and the old lady. And now I wish you to distinctly understand that I see clean through you both."

Saying this, he turned away from them and sauntered off with his hands in his pockets, his eyes flashing vengeance.

"I knew," said he, turning to them again, "that you had come here for no good. Wanted to buy me out, eh?"

They started away, and Moses, after mounting his horse, turned in his saddle and said, "We'll see who owns the property before we are through with you."

CHAPTER XXIX.—In the Meshes of the Law

W. L. Conklin and Isaac Deweese, candidates for the legislature, were to speak at the Haynes store on the next day after the visit of Moses Hopper and Frizzle to Dock Brown.

They proceeded to the place of speaking, where Moses delivered a letter of introduction to Mr. Conklin. Dock also was there. He saw Conklin in conversation with Moses and Frizzle. When it was ended he plucked the former to one side and in an excited manner asked, "What strangers are those? I never saw them before. They are wanting to buy mules, I believe?"

"It is possible," replied Conklin, "and as I am riding over the country a great deal, perhaps they supposed that I could give them some information."

Outlaw of Grayson County

The answer was indirect and hypothetical and gave Dock but little relief.

Moses and Frizzle retained Conklin as their attorney in the event of a suit against Dock for their interest in their father's and Pinkney's estate. And it was arranged that they should meet at Leitchfield the next day and consult further on the subject.

Feeling the pressure of recent developments, Dock went home and summoned to his aid all the wily wits of his mind to devise tricks and schemes of chicanery and villainy to meet and crush the inevitable exigencies rapidly crowding upon him. His first step was to visit the graves on the hill, where he picked and effaced the initial "H" from his father's name upon the monument above the grave of the latter in order to destroy the testimony it bore to the name of Hopper, doubtless saying to himself, "This letter was carved for the benefit of posterity and not for the benefit of the present generation."

He next rummaged among all the musty papers of the drawers and erased the name of Hopper wherever found. The notes and accounts in Pinkney's favor were indorsed with assignments and antedates—the dead man's name in imitation of his writing to each—a bill of sale for such property as the old man owned, all were in Dock's pockets—arms and equipment for the coming campaign.

The next day Moses and Frizzle came to Leitchfield, but learning that Mr. Conklin was at Grayson Springs, soon met him there. But the latter, feeling greater interest in politics than legal matters just then, requested Thomas Riley, a lawyer of Bardstown, who was visiting the Springs, to draft the petition. Mr. Riley did so. It is on file in the clerk's office of the Grayson Circuit Court, and begins:

"To the Honorable Judge of the Grayson Circuit Court, Sitting in Chancery: Your orators and oratrixes, Moses Hopper, Nathan Frizzle, and Annie, his wife, and Nancy Hopper, humbly complaining, respectfully state and charge that Gulliam Hopper, alias John Brown, departed this life in this circuit in May, 1848, intestate, ect."

The petition sets up an estate of $5,000 of which $3,000 is personalty and then reviews the history of the family from the killing of Stockstill, but charges that Pinkney was the moneyed man, and that he got his original capital from his father; and further charges that Dock had denied any and all relationship to his mother and other members of his family; and, further, that he has forged his father's and Pinkney's names to bills of sale and assignments on notes, etc., and, finally, prays for the writ of subpoena, the distribution of the property among the heirs, and for all equitable and general relief.

The writ of subpoena was issued by Esquires H. S. Bishop and B. L. Rogers, justices of the peace, upon the plaintiff's executing bond with Jack Thomas as surety. The writ was placed in the hands of Joseph Boone, sheriff, who proceeded to take the property into possession; but Dock called upon his friend, William Stinson, who became his surety for the forthcoming of the property attached, subject to the order of the court upon a final adjudication of the question involved in the suit.

Brown came to town, went to the clerk's office, read the petition, and then remarked to the parties present. ". . . that there never was such a damned put-up." Then with considerable gusto and forced humor said he would "make somebody smell a little hell before this suit was ended."

He spoke of John J. Thurman, a lawyer of Leitchfield, and employed him as an attorney. Thurman examined the petition and informed Brown that it was unnecessary to file an answer before court and that he could return home and depend upon his assistance in the defense.

The name of Hopper was now in everybody's mouth. The appearance of Moses and Frizzle in the county, the report of their relationship to Dock Brown, the institution of the suit, the allegations it contained, all made a bustle and stir among the people. But Brown's bold denial and self-assured manner when talking upon the subject induced some of quick credulity to believe his version of the story.

In order to forestall the probable influence a statement of the facts and circumstances would have upon Miss Ross and her parents if made by others, he hastened to their presence and jestingly disclosed them himself at the same time expressing great surprise that men should proceed to the extent of instituting an enormous suit upon a belief that he was their brother, when the fact was he was an entire stranger to them. Then, laughing, he said, "I should like to see the man who looks so much like me."

The Major and family also laughed when Dock assured them that there was nothing serious in the affair, and that it would soon blow over; adding that, for his part, he rather liked it, as it would cost him but little and prove to be a romance of some moment, terminating happily in a case of mistaken identity. Finding that his purpose at Ross's was accomplished, he bade the family good evening and went home, first having secured Miss Ross's consent for him to return early on the morning of the twenty-second of August and claim her as his own.

Stinson, who was on Dock's bond as surety, finally became uneasy and called upon Thurman for consolation. The latter expressed his faith in his client's integrity and said that he verily believed that Dock was sincere in his denial of the alleged relationship to the Hopper family.

"But there is one thing," he admitted, "which makes me fear sometimes that there is truth in the petition they have filed, and that is the very striking family resemblance the parties bear. Did you notice it?"

"Yes," said Stinson, "and this is what roused my suspicions. If Dock is not a brother of that man they call Hopper—Moses Hopper—they certainly must be nearly related, whether they know it or not. And Dock says if they are kin to him they are bastards, and he is going to say so in his answer. There is another thing in his favor," continued Stinson. "He says that he is willing, and in fact seems to be anxious, for you and me to go to Tennessee and make a full investigation of the whole matter, and thereby satisfy ourselves. This is a fair proposition, and before we condemn him we ought to give him a fair show. And he says further that he will furnish part of the money for our expenses."

"I'll go if you will," said Thurman.

"Agreed," said Stinson.

Dock had made his proposition to Stinson to allay his perceptible uneasiness and not with the slightest expectation that it would be accepted. So when the two called upon him to announce their readiness to proceed to Tennessee in accordance with his expressed desire, he was as much astonished as alarmed, and assured them that he did not have the money for their journey with him but would hand it to them on their return.

They journeyed down into Tennessee, met the Hopper family and were not long in satisfying themselves beyond all possibility of doubt that Dock's true name was Gulliam Hopper; that he was a brother of Moses, and in fact that everything charged in the petition was substantially true. The next object was to return and, if possible, to effect a compromise and smother the scandal which would inevitably result from its prosecution.

Upon their return to Leitchfield, on the twenty-second of August, they inquired for Dock and learned that he was married to Miss Ross that morning and had taken her to Pine Knob.

"It is, perhaps, well for him," said Stinson, "that the marriage was consummated before our return."

"Why?" asked Jacob Miller, the minister who officiated at the marriage.

"Nothing," said Thurman. Don't say any more, Uncle Billy. It will do no good and may do great harm."

The minister's curiosity was much excited but he walked away holding his peace.

Thurman and Stinson were annoyed by an inquisitive public, but made few disclosures except to Dock himself. Stinson was silent for the reason that he had hitherto taken a strong position in Dock's favor and against the protestations of many of his warm friends, and Thurman because he regarded his relation to the case and facts as purely professional, and such required an honorable silence.

Dock was not at all surprised at the report they made to him. Neither was he the least daunted, yet he pretended disbelief. With an expression upon his countenance of pleasurable expectation, he inquired:

"Isn't everything as I told you it was? Don't jest with me any longer."

"We don't jest," said Uncle Billy. "Certainly not in this instance. When your own character and that of others perhaps are involved, and public indignation aroused, do you suppose we would jest? We are only afraid to give utterance to the many painful facts we have gathered concerning you. But for the present I will leave you and Thurman to yourselves. Should you wish to see me again, you will generally find me at home. Good evening."

"Hold a moment, Uncle Billy!" exclaimed Dock. "You are not going away mad at me, I hope."

"No, I'm not mad," was the reply, "I am sorry for you and I don't thing I've got sense enough just now to talk to you. I'll see you again."

"Just a moment more," pleaded Dock, as the old gentleman started for the door again. "Promise me that you will come to no rash conclusion before you hear my side of the case. I don't blame you for present impressions, but then think what a great wrong you might do me by failing to hear my explanation."

Uncle Billy promised and went home.

"Now, Dock," said Thurman, "there can be nothing gained by trying to deceive me. I am your lawyer, and so far as it is consistent with honor and dignity, shall to the extent of my ability represent and protect your interests. And in order to this end it is necessary for me to be fully posted relative to your antecedents That is, all about yourself and family prior to your appearance at Pine Knob."

"Well," said Dock, "you are a lawyer and all that, and ought to know what's best; but I don't see that it is necessary for you to know anything further than my positive denial of being in any way related to any of those damned Hoppers, and that they have no right to any of the property I own. I was never at their house in my life, and know nothing about them. They've put up a big mess of lies, and now let 'em prove 'em if they can. But I think they'll have a tough time before they are through with Dock Brown. Isn't my denial all you want?"

"Well," said Thurman, "I suppose it is; for it is best for a lawyer never to be informed that his client is at all in the wrong. It is true in criminal cases, and I suppose the rule will hold in this instance."

The answer was filed denying every material allegation in the petition and charging that if the Hoppers were related to the defendant as brothers, they were unknown half-brothers and bastards, and that their mother was not his mother, and was never the wife of his father. Several amended petitions and answers and crosspetitions were soon filed, and the issue between the Hopper family and Dock Brown was fully made up. Thurman, McPherson, and Frank Peyton were Dock's lawyers, and John McHenry and W. L. Conklin represented the plaintiffs.

CHAPTER XXX Dock in Jail—His Attempt To Murder His Brother Moses

Shortly after Dock's answer was filed he was arrested upon the oath of Ab Hopper, charged with perjury. The examining trial was held at Leitchfield, and the charge being fully sustained, he was held to answer an indictment at the ensuing term of the circuit court. He was indicted, and the case being continued, he applied to the legislature for a charge of venue, Isaac Deweese, the representative from Grayson County, having presented and favored the bill. Accordingly the case was removed to Butler County.

Dock was incarcerated in jail. Mrs. Elizabeth Jackson, who still lives in Grayson County, was jailer, having been elected by the magistrates to fill the unexpired term of her deceased husband, William Jackson. Many of the neighbors and friends of the lady insisted upon her releasing her prisoner through fear that he might break his cell some night and kill her to prevent her thwarting his escape by raising an alarm. Such seemed to be the almost universal opinion of the man, inspired by his reckless bearing and reputation as a desperado. But she was not made of the stuff that is easily frightened out of the performance of duty, as the following incidents clearly prove:

One day she heard his sawing, sent out for assistance, and Dock was secured and placed in the dungeon. The saw was given him by Mr. S———, who lived in Hardin County at this time. He offered Mrs. Jackson one thousand dollars cash in hand to release Dock. Another man named W——— also came and, in company with S———, made another offer of a larger amount. But she refused all the proffered bribes. She permitted them, however, to ascend the stairs for the purpose of conversing with her prisoner and overheard them tell him they were suspected.

Dock then requested them to go to Pine Knob, get all the papers they could find, and bring them to him. They did so, and that night he called for some water. Mrs. Jackson had heard him walking in the outer prison near the trap-door, and being afraid to raise the door and furnish him with water, sent for Evan Rogers and John W. Gosnell to come and assist her; but before they arrived, her son, Andrew, and John J. McClure got Dock's dagger, which was downstairs, and, unlocking the trap-door, started up. Dock lifted the door and leaped over their heads. Mrs. Jackson was standing at the foot of the stairs and caught him by his long, bushy hair as he was rushing past her, and held him fast until her son and McClure came to her relief. Other persons from the town, hearing the alarm, came in, and Dock, begging for mercy, was carried to his old quarters and securely handcuffed by David McClure, others present refusing to rivet them on his wrist. He then offered several of the bystanders a sack of gold, which he had in his cell, if they would give him a knife and let him cut his throat.

"It's a damn disgrace," said he, "that a man who has as much money as I have should be handcuffed and kept in jail. Here's all of it for the man who will give a knife."

"I'll give it to you if you'll hand me the money and then cut your throat," said John R. Hackley.

But Dock refused to take the weapon thus offered on his own terms.

Outlaw of Grayson County

When the crowd left, he called Mrs. Jackson to the dungeon door. "Mrs. Jackson," he said, "you refused to take a thousand dollars to let me out of this place. Now I'll give you the whole bagful, which is over two thousand dollars, if you'll let me out. Besides, you are too nice a lady to be keeping jail; such an old barn of an affair as this, at any rate. Here, take it, and let me go free. That's a good and merciful woman!"

"I am sorry for you," she replied, "but it is my duty to keep you in here if I can; so it is no use for you to offer me money or anything else." Saying which, she went downstairs.

Mrs. Dock Brown in the meantime had returned to her father and made frequent trips to the jail until she was taken sick. Dock was now transferred to jail at Morgantown. Mrs. Brown, learning this, sent for Uncle Billy Stinson, whim she regarded as Dock's friend, and requested him, for her sake, to go on his bond, that he might be with her during the dreadful ordeal through which she must pass. Stinson was moved by her entreaties and executed the bond for Dock's appearance at the next term of Butler Circuit Court.

The child was born and christened James Ross. "He lived, moved, and had his being" at and in the vicinity of Leitchfield, and will be mentioned again.

James House and Dock went to the Butler Circuit Court together. On the way Dock remarked to his companion, "If I can only get Moses out of the way, I've got enough charges against Ab Hopper to keep him away from court forever."

They reached Morgantown and stopped at Howard's Hotel, and while sitting in the public room, Moses entered with a musket in his hand, rubbed it against Dock and asked the crowd if they had "seen anything of these damned Hoppers about here?"

Brink Neal said, "Yes, I suppose you are one of them."

"Yes, and there's some more of the damned stock around here," replied Moses.

The case of the Commonwealth vs. Dock Brown for perjury was called and continued on motion of the defendant.

Moses Hopper and other witnesses for the prosecution had started for their homes.

Dock's witnesses were at dinner. He was out. Presently there was a scream heard in Mrs. Howard's apartment. The guests rushed in and found Moses, wounded and bleeding, in the hands of friends. He was shot in the back, but the wound was not necessarily fatal.

"Who did it?" was the general inquiry.

"Dock Brown," said Moses. "As soon as I was shot I snapped back at the place like a bear and saw Dock run off. He's the very damn rascal who done it."

A few minutes later, Dock made his appearance in the public room, his pants bristling with Spanish needles and torn at the knee. He was turning the key to his watch with careless indifference. When some one asked him if he had heard of the shooting, he replied indifferently that he had not. He then repaired to the court house, where he took a seat immediately in front of Colonel Alfred Allen who then was Commonwealth's Attorney. Colonel Allen noticed that he appeared to be making tremendous exertions to suppress nervous excitement. Great drops of perspiration fell off his head and neck like rain. Colonel Allen called the attention of several sitting near him to the fact, and wondered what had excited him, not having heard of the shooting of Moses.

Judge Calhoun, who occupied the bench, was informed of the circumstance and, looking over at Dock, remarked:

"Mr. Brown, you are suspected of having shot Moses Hopper. Consider yourself under arrest. Mr. Sheriff, you will take charge of Mr. Brown and hold him until further orders from this court."

Moses was bandaged around the breast, and being stripped to the waist, except the bandage, mounted his horse and rode through the streets of Morgantown, crying out that he was shot and perhaps killed, but he could whip Dock Brown or any of his friends.

Brink Neal said, "Turn Dock Brown loose and let 'em kill each other, and then pitch 'em both over a bluff, damn 'em."

Next day Dock was returned to the Leitchfield jail for safe keeping, the Morgantown jail being regarded as insecure. He was soon bailed out by his friend, Stinson, and others.

CHAPTER XXXI
More Suits—Dock's Rascality—Probable Murder of Sam Hopper

Samuel Hopper had removed to Perry County, Illinois, and was residing there at the time of his father's death, Pinkney's and James's deaths; but of the latter he did not hear until eighteen hundred and fifty, and then it was mere rumor. His information was derived from the girl in Warrick County, Indiana, who had kept house for James prior to his departure for Kentucky. She told Sam, who still retained his lawful name of Hopper, that she had no doubt in the world of his being dead, for he had promised to return within two weeks and arrange some business matters of importance which she knew he would not neglect. "And now," said she, "it has been two years and over since he and his little boy left, and I have not heard a word from either of them. He sold his house and farm to his brothers, one of whom was over here with him."

Sam had gone to Warrick County to see James, but received the above information and returned home, and in conversation with a lawyer relative to his interest in Pinkney's estate, which he regarded as being by no means meager, he disclosed the true names of all and some circumstances which led the lawyer to identify Pinkney as the man who had swindled his friend, Grubbs, of Montgomery County, Kentucky, with which circumstance he had become acquainted through a letter from Grubbs some years before. He immediately wrote to the latter, informing him of what he had heard, stating that he entertained no doubt that the man who died in Grayson County, Kentucky, under the name of Pinkney H. Brown, was the some person who had embezzled his money.

Grubbs came immediately to Grayson, saw Dock Brown, and at once identified him as the young man who had been at his house with Pinkney Hooper, and was regarded there as his brother. Grubbs spoke to him, addressing him as Hooper, but Dock replied:

"You are mistaken, I guess, sir. That is not my name."

"What, then, is your name, if you please?" asked Grubbs.

"Brown, sir," was the reply.

"Ugh! Ugh!" grunted Grubbs. "You don't know me, eh?"

"No, sir," said Dock, "and since you are so impudent, I don't want to know you; that's more of it."

"Well, we will not fuss about it," said Grubbs. "But I reckon you will know me before I get through with you."

They then separated.

At this time the suit of the Hopper heirs had been progressing for about two years. The estates of John Brown, alias Hopper, deceased, were ordered into the hands of Sheriff Joseph Boone as public administrator. The prosecution against Dock for perjury and malicious shooting and wounding were still pending, being continued from term to term.

On the twenty-eighth of June, eighteen hundred and fifty, Thomas Grubbs filed his "Bill in Chancery," setting up at length his first acquaintance with the Hopper family in Montgomery County, the reputation they bore there, his confidence in Pinkney's honesty, the subsequent betrayal, the extent of swindle and embezzlement, Pinkney's concealment, his present belief in an accidental discovery of the same family (represented in the person of Dock Brown), and property accumulated by his (complainant's) own capital. He concluded as follows:

"In tender consideration of the premises, and being without remedy at law, he prays your honor to take cognizance of his case, and grant him relief. He prays that the said estate left by said Pinkney may be applied to the payment of the amount due to your orator. That the defendants answer this bill on oath as specifically as though the allegations thereof were repeated by way of interrogatory. He prays the writ of subpoena, and for such other and further relief as to equity belongs, and as in duty bound he will ever pray, etc. Samuels, for Complainant."

At the next term of court Grubbs's suit, which included his original bill and numerous amendments, was consolidated with the Hopper suit, also with the suit of John Finley's heirs, of Scott County, which was filed in eighteen hundred and fifty, seeking to recover from the Browns', alias Hoppers', estate five hundred acres of land. The petition charged that on the sixteenth of March, seventeen hundred and ninety-one, a patent was issued from the Commonwealth of Virginia to one Robert Forman, and by Forman conveyed to their testator, John Finley, who paid the taxes on same land until his death in eighteen hundred and twenty-three, and then his heirs, being infants, failed to list and pay taxes on same; that the land was forfeited for non-payment of taxes. But in eighteen hundred and fifty they paid all taxes, interests, and cost thereon and redeemed the land. They further charged that John Brown, alias Hopper, deceased, had purchased the land of Jack Thomas, Esq., agent for the Commonwealth, and that Dock Brown was then in possession, claiming same as sole heir of his deceased father.

The three consolidated suits were now in full blast. Hon. Jesse H. Kincheloe, of Hardinsburg, was the circuit judge. The pleading, processes, orders, etc., are numerous and voluminous, and of a

Outlaw of Grayson County

novel and very extraordinary character, involving many exceedingly nice points in law and equity; but insomuch as the general reader would not appreciate the labyrinthian difficulties of such a suit if presented in full and specifically, it is deemed only proper, in connection with the outline of facts already written, to mention a few occasional orders, and at the proper time the final judgment of the court and ultimate disposition of the case.

William Stinson had taken a mortgage upon the Negroes and most of the personalty as indemnity against loss as Dock's surety in penal bonds, etc. The court, however, regardless of these mortgages, ordered the personalty to be sold and Negroes hired out, and the money to be collected by Edwin Thomas, commissioner, and held by him subject to the order of court.

These orders were made immediately preceding the fall term of the Butler Circuit Court, wherein both criminal prosecutions against Dock were pending. So he was soon making active preparations for a clandestine departure to parts unknown. His wife was yet at her father's in Leitchfield and refused to live with him longer. The Major had also closed his doors against him. He had made several unsuccessful attempts, through Jake Brazier, to get possession of his little boy, who was now two years old. He finally told Brazier that he would have the boy if he had to kill everything in the county to get him.

The courts were too near at hand for him to delay longer. With Brazier's assistance, he, Ambrose and Letitia were in a spring wagon at dusk, starting for Missouri — Dock and Ambrose in female, and Letitia, in male, apparel, disguised as peddlers. They crossed the Ohio next morning at sunrise. He made the trip to Missouri with his one-horse spring wagon, sold the Negroes, realizing fifteen hundred dollars for the two; loitered and dissipated around for a few months, then stole Letitia and brought her to Memphis, Tennessee, where he sold her again for eight hundred dollars. She was a bright, and many say, beautiful mulatto, and for this reason Dock treated her more as a companion than slave, and had no difficulty in kidnapping her. At each sale he promised to return and get her, provided she would not betray him. But after selling her in Memphis he left for Kentucky and saw her no more.

Charles Wortham Sr., who had succeeded Boone as sheriff, made affidavit to the fact that Dock Brown had stolen two of the Negroes ordered to be hired out, and that owing to this fact the people would not hire the others, through fear of their being stolen and their employers secretly damaged. Upon the presentation of this affidavit in court, Lucy, her children, and Sam were ordered to be sold. Wortham made the sale by public outcry at the court house door in Leitchfield. Ab Hopper became the purchaser of all, and took them to his home in Tennessee, near Chalk Bluff, on the Mississippi River.

About this time Samuel Hopper came to Grayson County, looking after his interest in the suits pending. He met with Brazier, and the two spent most of their nights at the Pine Knob home. Jake went to the spring one night and there met Dock, who came to the house and met Sam. The three talked nearly all night, but before day Dock was among the hills. Brazier carried food to him and his horse for several days. At length, Sam Hopper was missed from the county and has never been heard of since. His horse was afterward sold at Hawesville by Dock. He disappeared and left no sign. If living, his course baffled the knowledge of everyone. If dead, no evidence of the fact ever manifested itself. His family in Illinois wrote letters of inquiry, but the answers were uniform, and in substance that he had gone from the county, but when or where no one seemed to know. Of course, the most rational conclusion is that he was murdered by Dock Brown. Brazier said that the last he saw of him he was on his horse, and stated that he was going back to his family in Illinois.

CHAPTER XXXII
A Fatal Duel in the Woods—Exit of Ab Hopper and Dock Brown

Dock Brown, after his return from the South, was seldom visible and then to but a few persons. He made his temporary home with Martin Edwards, his cousin, in Ohio County, but was always on the lookout for pursuers. He offered Mart four hundred dollars in cash to go with him to Ab Hopper's residence in Tennessee and get Lucy to meet him in the woods back of the farm and run off with him. Edwards accepted the offer with the understanding that if he failed in inducing Lucy to meet him, the money should be refunded, reserving his expenses.

The first night of their journey they slept by a bright fire. Edwards said, speaking of it long afterward, that about one or two o'clock in the morning he awoke from some unaccountable cause and saw Dock slipping on tiptoe toward him with his bowie knife in hand. "I sprang up instantly," said he, "and asked him what he was aiming to do. But he replied that he didn't know, but that he reckoned he had a spell on him. I told him he must not have any more such spells, for if he did, I might have a worse one. He had

Outlaw of Grayson County

concluded, doubtless, that I was going to betray him, and his evident intention was to kill me."

They had a gun and pistol each. Dock's gun was the same rifle with which his father had killed Stockstill.

Reaching the vicinity of Ab's farm, Dock concealed himself in the top of a tree-lap, while Edwards went to the house, where he was received by Ab with friendly greetings. His horse was put away and fed for the night. He saw Lucy and spoke to her but had no opportunity at the time to deliver Dock's message. Watching every movement, he saw her at the woodyard picking up chips in her apron. It was in the direction of the stable, and he started to the latter place with the intention of dropping a word as he passed. But Ab called to him to wait and he would accompany him. Thus his effort was foiled for the time. The morning of the next day was nearly gone when Ab's family physician, Dr. Boone, called to take dinner with him. He was introduced to Edwards, and after a brief conversation, the doctor remarked to Ab that he wanted to see him on a little private business. Requesting Mart to keep his seat and make himself at home, Ab walked out to the gate with the doctor, got his horse and led him to the stable, the two men conversing in a low tone as they went.

Edwards, deeming this his opportunity, went to the kitchen and acquainted Lucy with his business and Dock's locality, telling her that she should have fifty dollars as soon as she would meet Dock, but advised her not to make the attempt until night. She consented to go at the time designated.

The doctor had seen Dock from the blind path he had just traveled. Dock also saw him, but neither spoke. This aroused the doctor's suspicions and was the subject of the private conversation with Ab who seemed to identify the man in the woods intuitively and was at no loss to fathom the object of his presence. He came to the house, took his gun from the rack, and deliberately walked off in the direction of the place designated by the doctor. He came to the tree-top but found nothing but traces of where a man and horse had gone. Following the tracks for a hundred yards or more along a dim path, he saw a horse hitched, with head near the ground, some two hundred yards on ahead. It was hitched to keep it from neighing. He stooped and crawled cautiously in the direction of the animal. He had not gone far until his path led him by the edge of a large and deep sink hole. Something down there attracted his attention. He glanced down and saw Dock who stood with gun presented. Ab instantly raised his weapon, and both fired and fell. Dock was shot in the face, the ball entering his brain. Ab was shot in the abdomen.

The reports were heard at the house, and Mart Edwards, who had been restlessly walking in the yard ever since Ab went out with his gun, remarked to the doctor that somebody was killed by those shots. The doctor seemed to be impressed with the same idea, and together they hurried with all speed to the scene of the fearful double tragedy.

Ab and Dock were both down, the latter insensible and speechless. Ab's eldest daughter came out and, seeing Dock, jumped up and down upon him until life was extinct and then, clenching her hands in his hair, dragged the body from the sink hole.

"Let the poor body alone; it's done its course," said Ab.

When the doctor told Ab that he must die too, he remarked, "I don't care, as I have killed that damned rascal."

He died that night at nine o'clock.

Martin Edwards was arrested the same day, charged with being accessory to the murder and put under guard at Ab Hopper's house. He was upstairs and, watching his opportunity, sprang from a window and made his escape, returning to his home in Kentucky. He became a good and reputable citizen, and furnished the above details of Dock Brown's death to the writer's informant.

Ab and Dock were buried in a country graveyard. the remains of the latter were deposited in an obscure corner, with no friend by to water his grave with the tears of sympathy or regret. A rough stone at the head alone marks the spot, upon which is simply written, "Gulliam Hopper."

CHAPTER XXXIII The End of it All.

The following is an extract from Judge Kincheloe's opinion and judgment, entered of record at the April term, 1856, in the three consolidated suits:

"The facts exhibited in this record present a sad picture of human nature under the debasing influence of unrestrained selfishness and cupidity, springing up incidentally in the course of an investigation of the civil rights of the parties. They embody a catalogue of atrocious acts which has but few parallels in the annals of crime.

"In the earlier history of the parties to this record the father of the complainants and defendant in the first suit slew a man in Tennessee. His brother, Moses, one in Indiana, each fled from justice and, having wandered about from place to place, finally settled and met in Grayson County under assumed names. Gulliam Brown, or Hopper, was afterward slain by the defendant, his own son, who was afterward slain in Tennessee by his brother, who also died of a mortal wound received in the combat.

"Homicide, however, is not the only species of crime displayed on the record. Imposition, fraud, embezzlement, perjury, attempted perjury, fabrication of false proof, abound in the facts and pleading in the cases.

"The answer of Gulliam Hopper Jr. contains as many falsehoods as were ever spread on the same quantity of paper. Glaring, palpable falsehoods, so easily susceptible of confutation, they almost challenge belief from their boldness. Falsehoods, too, of the most extraordinary character—falsely denying not only his brothers and sisters, but the mother that bore him, an offense as startling on account of its unnaturalness as of its criminality. The preparation of his case in the county is consistent with his pleadings. A pretended will is exhibited with a view to procure proof as to handwriting. A paper purporting to be a bill of sale is exhibited and then suppressed. False claims are endeavored to be procured, together with other tricks and devices. The conduct and conversation of such a man cannot be truly interpreted by the rules applied to the transactions of common men. Ordinarily, men speak and act truthfully and honestly; and we thus interpret their actions. But this record places the defendant in the attitude of a false, dishonest man; and his actions must be interpreted accordingly.

". . . the Hoppers have established heirship to the estates of Pinkney H. and John, or Gulliam, Brown, or Hopper, and are therefore entitled to their distributive shares of these estates, after payment of debts. But it is manifest that nothing will be left for distribution.

". . . It is rather remarkable that the resistance of the defendant, Gulliam Brown, or Hopper, to the claims of his relatives as distributees of his brother's and father's estates, and the litigation which followed, led indirectly to the institution of the suit of Grubbs vs. Brown, which will absorb the whole fund in contest between the relatives."

The opinion and judgment embrace many pages of the record, reviewing the whole of the case, deciding in favor of Grubbs to the extent of his claim, and ordering sales and collections for his benefit out of Pinkney's estate; also sustaining the claim of the Finley heirs to the five hundred acres of land. But before the final termination of the suits, Grubbs and Moses Hopper died, and the money collected—amounting to over four thousand, five hundred dollars—was paid to the heirs of the former. The cases were stricken from the docket of the Grayson Circuit Court in the year eighteen hundred and seventy-three, having been there twenty-five years.

The End.

APPENDIX

Jim Ross, alias Brown, alias Hopper, was a school boy in Leitchfield in eighteen hundred and sixty-two. None of his schoolmates have forgotten the chubby, round-faced, gray-eyed, pug-nosed lad, about twelve years old. He was as unbridled and free from parental control as an adult. He didn't like boys—seldom associated or played with them—but would sit in a crowd of men and look upon juvenile sports as of "the long ago" with him, too. In a word, he seemed to feel that he was a man and took an interest in the conversation only of men. He always carried a little pistol. All of the school boys knew this but none dared inform the teacher, for Jim had threatened to kill the first boy who should thus betray him; and none doubted that he would be as good as his word in this regard; consequently, he carried the weapon for a month or two before Professor W. B. Hayward found it out. The discovery was by accident. He had been tampering with it in time of books, when it slipped from his hand and fell upon the floor. The professor saw it and very excitedly asked:

"Whose pitsol is that?"

The boys, with pleasure, seemed to feel that the crisis had come. There was no answer, but a dead silence reigned.

"I asked, whose pistol is that," exclaimed the professor with an

Outlaw of Grayson County

earnest look toward the neighborhood of Jim's desk. Every eye in the school was upon Jim, who seemed carelessly gazing upon his open book. The professor, taking all in at a glance, advanced rapidly toward the pistol. But before he reached it, Jim deliberately picked it up and put it in his pocket.

"Give that here," demanded Professor Hayward. Jim didn't move a muscle or make answer. The professor, being almost exasperated, put his hand upon Jim's closely-shorn head, gave it a fearful shake, saying:

"Do you hear me, sir?"

But Jim was still silent.

The professor then took him by the arm, jerked him from his seat, and took the pistol away from him.

"Now, be seated there, and I will settle with you at noon." Saying which, the professor turned to other matters. As he walked away, Jim looked around at his fellow-students, put his thumb on the end of his nose, and gave his hand a twist at the teacher, as much to say, "O, no; I guess not."

He was no nearer conquered than at first, and was doubtless the only pupil Professor Hayward ever failed to conquer upon the spot when he deemed it necessary. In this particular case, he very wisely chose a different plan from that which was expected from the remainder of the school.

The other pupils were dismissed at noon, but the professor and Jim remained. What was said and done none of us ever learned, but about a quarter of an hour afterward they came up town together, and Jim came to school as before, but without his little pistol. There lives no better judge of human nature than Professor Hayward, and it was the general impression that he had come to the conclusion that harsh means would be inadequate to the task and had adopted mild ones, with remarkable success, for they never had any further trouble, and Jim's schoolmates were much relieved.

Strangers often wondered at the familiarity with which Jim addressed grown persons, calling them by their Christian names, without a title, and why, with his graceful (?) oaths, his presence was tolerated. But those who knew him well understood what it was, because people, even grown ones, were afraid to give him the slightest rebuff. His acquaintances had all heard him threaten the life of some person. He used to say:

"My daddy killed his daddy, and, by God, I am going to kill granddaddy. I'll cut his throat from ear to ear, damn him!" His grandfather was very hard of hearing and used an ear-trumpet. Jim would talk mildly to the old gentleman through this and then curse him without it. For instance, in the trumpet, he would say, "Yes, granddaddy, I'll attend to it," and then, aside, "You damned old toothless miser, I'd see you in hell first."

I remember on one occasion, when Professor W. B. Hayward was lecturing the school upon some moral question, as was his wont to do, and he remarked that he was sorry to say that he had heard of some profanity amongst his pupils. "One in particular," said he. "You, James Ross; I have been much pained to learn that you are profane."

"You heard a damned lie," said Jim, in an undertone.

"But," continued the professor," "I am glad to say to your credit that I never heard you use an oath. And although I am extremely sorry to learn that you should at any time be guilty of such immorality, you have had the respect for me never to have used any improper language in my presence."

No such disrespect was ever expected from any other source, for Prof. W. B. Hayward had, and still has, the happy faculty of ingratiating himself into the affections of his pupils, whose gratitude to him will only perish with their memories.

Jim Ross never studied his books of nights but, with a bottle of whiskey and a deck of cards, would go to the woods and gamble all night upon money purloined from the bar-room drawer. His mother, grandfather and half-sister, Mima (born out of wedlock), were the only occupants of the hotel up to 1863, to which time it retained the reputation of being the best hotel in Kentucky, notwithstanding the fact that Jim's mother had given birth to Mima and figured extensively in a bastardy prosecution in the Grayson County Court.

But Jake Brazier came to town and was employed by the Major to keep bar, the Major being too old and Jim being too reckless and familiar with the money-drawer for his services in this capacity to be at all profitable to the Major. How such a reckless man as Brazier succeeded in insinuating himself into the good graces of the Major was strange to the people who knew them both. But it is probable that no one had ever told him of the intimate relation existing between Jake and Dock Brown. For a time the Major seemed highly pleased with Jake's services, as was also Mrs. Brown, whose smiles and kind attentions to Jake soon ripened into———.

They married with the Major's consent. Jake was put in charge of the whole premises. But the Major never knew that Jim was full master of the situation—that he could say to Brazier, "Stand there!" and he would stand; "Go there!" and he would go. This was the

Outlaw of Grayson County

case. Jim could crook his finger, and Jake's mouth would fly open like a shot-trap. Yet toward others Jake appeared to be as game as a muskrat.

The two were well matched and were soon full partners in villainy. They handled the bar stock, its capital and profits; the Major, the hotel money.

Thus matters went on for about a year, when the poor old Major died. He was buried upon his own lot, near the hotel. What money he left, outsiders have never been able to learn, yet it is supposed that it ran up into the thousands, and that Jake and Jim got hold of it all. They still kept the hotel, but the leading spirit had passed away; and with him the good name of the house. Only the traveling public from a distance ever stopped there, and those but once, for it was soon known that the house was turned into a gambling hall, and the proprietors were the principal operators. Those who visited the house went for drinks and games. For a time the proprietors were greatly the losers. But such was not long to continue. They opened a little trap-door in the floor overhead. Here of evenings before the gamblers arrived one (generally Jim), would take his stand with a deck of cards. The game would be made up, and Jake had only to throw his eyes up in a careless way to learn from Jim the kind of hand he was playing against. This was quite a success for a long time. But on one occasion Jim failed to show his hand distinctly, from some cause, and Jake peeping up too long, was discovered, and the game broke up in a row. And thus one of their principal means of living was virtually ended.

There was some petty thieving going on in and around Leitchfield, and the eye of suspicion was not infrequently directed toward Jake Brazier and Jim Ross—the latter always went by the name of Ross, as did his mother after Dock Brown's villainy became notorious.

Jake, like his old preceptor, Dock Brown, would frequently leave the county for weeks at a time and return with some fine horses and sell them in Grayson. This was carried on with success for a year or more, and it was not found out that the animals had been stolen by him in the state of Ohio until after he left the county never to return. He was arrested and held by an examining court in Grayson to answer the charge of robbery committed upon the person of one Lewis Duggin, a good citizen of Grayson, whom Jake had overdosed with whiskey, and whilst Duggin was in a state of intoxication, rifled his pockets, taking $180. He gave bond, but before the next term of court he and Jim Ross were caught in

DOCK BROWN

Jack Roger's meat house stealing bacon. They were arrested and put under guard but made their escape. Jake was not heard from for several years afterward when a letter came stating that he was dead. Jim wandered abroad for a few years until at length he boarded a steamboat between Louisville and Owensboro. An acquaintance of his from Grayson having got aboard the boat at Cloverport, saw him. It was midwinter, and the Ohio was almost gorged with ice. Jim, finding that his acquaintance had made him the center of attraction amongst the passengers, and being afraid of arrest, went on the hurricane deck and sauntered about for a time, when presently his acquaintance and a few others stepped up for the purpose of interviewing him. They passed a few compliments before the acquaintance asked Jim if he didn't want to go back to Grayson. Jim thought the hour for his arrest was at hand, but he walked backward to the stern before he answered:

"No," he said, "I'll go to hell first, and here goes!" Saying which, he sprang from the boat, feet foremost, amongst the floating ice and disappeared forever.

Emma Ross and her daughter, Mima, left Grayson County shortly after Jake and Jim. They took up their humble abode in the state of Illinois. Mima soon returned and remained in and around Leitchfield for a time. Seldom have I seen a more beautiful countenance than hers. It seemed clothed with the vesture of heavenly innocence and purity. Her form was lovely, and she also seemed to be the embodiment of grace and modesty. But, alas! like "the beautiful blue butterfly of Cashmere," whose golden pinions the beetle touches

"Gayer butterflies glittering by
Ne'er droop their wings o'er those that die."

Since writing this story, she and her mother have both passed into the spirit world. And may my pen, nor yours, dear reader, ever unmantle the faults of injured woman, be she living or dead.

www.ingramcontent.com/pod-product-compliance
Lightning Source LLC
Chambersburg PA
CBHW052100110526
44591CB00013B/2289